THE NEW STONE AGE
IN NORTHERN EUROPE

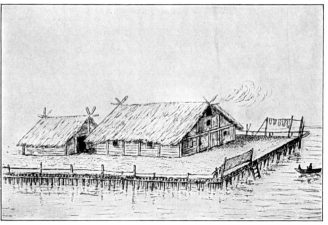

RECONSTRUCTED LAKE-DWELLINGS

THE NEW STONE AGE
IN NORTHERN EUROPE

BY

JOHN M. TYLER

PROFESSOR EMERITUS OF BIOLOGY, AMHERST COLLEGE

LONDON
G. BELL AND SONS, Lᴛᴅ.
1921

𝕿𝖔

JOSEPH DÉCHELETTE

PATRIOT AND ARCHÆOLOGIST

KILLED IN BATTLE AT VINGRÉ (AISNE)

OCTOBER 3, 1914

PREFACE

THE dawn of history came late in Northern Europe and the morning was stormy. We see the Roman Empire struggling in vain to hold back successive swarms of barbarians, pouring from a dim, misty, mysterious northland. Centuries of destruction and confusion follow; then gradually states and institutions emerge, and finally our own civilization, which, though still crude and semibarbarous, has its glories as well as its obvious defects.

The growth, development, and training of these remarkable destroyers and rebuilders was slowly going on through the ages of prehistoric time. Most of the germs, and many of the determinants, of our modern institutions and civilization can be recognized in the habits, customs, and life of the Neolithic period. Hence the importance of its study to the historian and sociologist. It has left us an abundance of records, if we can decipher and interpret them. It opens with savages living on shell-heaps along the Baltic. Later we find the stone monuments of the dead rising in France, England, Scandinavia, and parts of Germany. They begin as small rude shelters and end as temples, like that at Stonehenge. People were thinking and co-operating, and there must have been no mean social organization.

We find agriculture highly developed in the valleys of the Danube and its tributaries. We see villages erected on piles along the shores of the Swiss lakes — probably a later development. We find implements, pottery, and bones of animals; charred grains of wheat and barley and loaves of bread; cloth and ornaments — almost a complete inventory of the food and furnishings of the people of this period. We should call them highly civilized, had they been able to write their own history. What was their past and whence had they come?

Implements and pottery tell us of exchange of patterns and ideas, or may suggest migrations of peoples, and finally map out long trade-routes. Some day the study of the pottery will give us a definite chronology, but not yet.

We can reconstruct, to some extent, these phases of prehistoric life. Our greatest difficulties begin when we attempt to combine these separate parts in one pattern or picture, to trace their chronological succession or the extent of their overlappings and their mutual influence and relations in custom and thought. Here, we admit, our knowledge is still very vague and inadequate. Twenty years ago the problem seemed insoluble; perhaps it still remains so. But during that time explorations, investigations, and study have given us many most important facts and suggestions. Some inferences we can accept with a fair degree of confidence, others have varying degrees of probability, sometimes we can only guess. But guesses do no harm, if acknowledged and recognized as such.

I venture to hope that historian and sociologist may find valuable facts and suggestions in this book. But, while writing it, I have thought more often of the eager young student who may glance over its pages, feel the allurement of some topic and resolve to know more about it. The bibliography is prepared especially for him. It is anything but complete. The literature of the period is almost endless. I have referred to only a few of the best and most suggestive works. They will introduce him to a chain of others. If he studies their facts and arguments he will probably reject some of my opinions or theories, modify others, and form his own. If I can do any young student this service, my work will

have been amply repaid. America has sent few
laborers into this rich harvest field.

I wish that this little book might play the
part of a good host, and introduce many intelligent, thoughtful, and puzzled readers to the
company and view-point of the prehistorian.

In prehistory we find man entering upon
course after course of hard and rigid discipline
and training, usually under the spur of necessity, the best of all teachers. Every course lasts
through millennia. Their chief end is to socialize and humanize individual men. Environment, natural or artificial, is a means to this end.
It compels men to struggle, each with himself;
only as men improve is any marked change of
conditions possible or desirable. Men must
"pass" in the lower course before they can be
promoted to the next higher, to find here a
similar field of struggle on a somewhat higher
plane. Human evolution, as a process of hu-
manizing and socializing man, is and must be
chiefly ethical; for ethics is nothing more nor
less than the science and art of living rightly
with one's neighbor. And man is incurably religious, always feeling after the power or powers
in or behind nature, whose essential character
she is compelling him to express, as her inadequate but only mouthpiece. He will gradually

become like what he is feeling after, dimly recognizing, and rudely worshipping. These are
the most important departments of the school
of prehistoric man.

The story told us by the evolutionist and prehistorian is full of surprises. It tells us of the
failure of dominant species of animals and of
promising races of men. It shows men plodding
wearily through hardship and discouragement,
and finding therein the road to success. The
apparently dormant peoples and periods often
prove in the end to have been those of most
rapid advance. "The race is not to the swift
nor the battle to the strong." But it enables us
to plot the line of human progress by points far
enough apart to allow us to distinguish between
minor and temporary oscillations and fluctua-
tions and the law of the curve. The torch is
passed from people to people and from continent to continent, but never falls or goes out.
There is always a "saving remnant." We have
grounds for a reasonable hope, not of a millennium, but of success in struggle. The econo-
mist, sociologist, and even the historian, are
lookouts on the ship; evolution and prehistory
must furnish chart and compass, and tell us
our port of destination.

Many or most of the best thoughts in this

book are borrowed. Some of these borrowings are credited to their owners in the bibliography. Of many others I can no longer remember the source. The recollection of successive classes of students in Amherst College, with whom I have discussed these topics, will always be a source of inspiration and gratitude. I owe many valuable suggestions to my colleagues in the faculty, especially to Professor F. B. Loomis. To the unfailing kindness and ability of Mr. and Miss Erb, of the Library of Columbia University; to Professor H. F. Osborn for his generous hospitality; to the staff of the Boston Public Library; to Doctor L. N. Wilson, of the Library of Clark University; most of all, to Mr. R. L. Fletcher and his assistants, of the Library of Amherst College, my debt is greater than can be expressed in any word of thanks.

CONTENTS

xiii

CONTENTS

CONTENTS

ILLUSTRATIONS

MAP

THE NEW STONE AGE IN
NORTHERN EUROPE

The first of the two numbers and the letter in the foot-notes designate the position in the Bibliography at the end of the volume of the title referred to; the second refers to the page of the book or article.

THE NEW STONE AGE IN NORTHERN EUROPE

CHAPTER I

THE COMING OF MAN

MAN has been described as a "walking museum of paleontology." He is like a mountain whose foundations were laid in a time so ancient that even the paleontologist hardly finds a record to decipher; whose strata testify to the progress of life through all the succeeding ages; whose surface, deeply ploughed by the glaciers, is clothed with grass and forest, flower and fruit, the harvest of the life of to-day.

Some of his organs are exceedingly old, while others are but of yesterday; yet all are highly developed in due proportion, knit and harmonized in a marvellously tough, vigorous, adaptable body, the instrument of a thinking and willing mind. Most surviving animals have outlived their day of progress; they have "exhausted their lead," to borrow a miner's expression, and have settled down in equilibrium with their surroundings. But discontented man is wisely convinced that his golden age lies in the future, and that his best possessions are his hopes and dreams, his castles in Spain. He is chiefly a bundle of vast possibilities, of great expectations, compared with which his achievements and realizations are scarcely larger than the central point of a circle compared with its area.

Physically he belongs to the great branch or phylum of vertebrate animals having a backbone — sometimes only a rod of cartilage — an internal locomotive skeleton, giving the possibility of great strength and swiftness, and of large size. Large size, with its greater heat-producing mass relative to its radiating surface, implies the possibility of warm blood, or constant high temperature, resulting in greater activity of all the organs, especially of the glands and the nervous system. Large size, as a rule, is accompanied by long life — giving opportunities for continuous and wide experience, and hence for intelligence. Yet most vertebrates have remained cold-blooded, and only a "saving remnant" even of men is really intelligent. Man belongs to the highest class of vertebrates, the Mammals, which produce living young and suckle them. Among the highest mammals, the Primates, or apes, the length of the periods of gestation, of suckling the young, and of childhood, with its dependence upon the mother, have become so long that she absolutely requires some sort of help and protection from the male parent. From this necessity have sprung various grades and forms of what we may venture to call family life, with all its advantages. How many mammals have attained genuine family life and how many men have realized its possibilities?[1]

The upward march of our ancestors was neither easy nor rapid. They were anything but precocious. They were always ready to balk at progress, stiff-necked creatures who had to be driven and sternly held in the line of progress by stronger competitors. The ancestors of vertebrates maintained the swimming habit, which resulted in the development of the internal skeleton and finally of a backbone, not because it was easiest or most desirable, but because any who went to the rich feeding-grounds of the sea-bottom were eaten up by the mollusks and crabs. Our earliest air-breathing ancestors were crowded toward, and finally to the land, and into air-breathing by the pressure of stronger marine forms like sharks, or by climatic changes.[2] Reptiles, not mammals, domi-

[1] 16, 17.   [2] 1: 477; 671, chap. XXIX.

nated the earth throughout the Mesozoic era, and harried our ancestors into agility and wariness; at a later period the apes remained in the school of arboreal life mainly because the ground was forbidden and policed by the Carnivora. They and their forebears were compelled to forego some present ease and comfort, but always kept open the door to the future.

In spite of all this vigorous policing, malingerers and deserters turned aside from the upward line of march at every unguarded point or fork in the road, escaped from the struggle, and settled down in ease and stagnation or degeneration, like our very distant cousins, the monkeys and lower apes. Long-continued progress is a marked exception, not the rule, in the animal world, and is maintained only by the "saving remnant." And these continue to progress mainly because Nature is "always a-chivying of them and a-telling them to move on," as Poor Joe said of Detective Bucket, and her guiding wand is the spur of necessity.

The Primates, or apes, are, as we have seen, the highest order of the great class of mammals. Most of them, like other comparatively defenseless vertebrates, are gregarious or even social.[1] They have a feeling of kind, if not of kindness,

[1] 18.

toward one another. This sociability, together with the family as a unit of social structure, has contributed incalculably to human intellectual and moral development. Man is a Primate, a distant cousin of the highest apes, though no one of these represents our "furry arboreal ancestor with pointed ears." Arboreal life was an excellent preparatory training toward human development. Our primate ancestor was probably of fair size. In climbing he set his feet on one branch and grasped with his hands the branch above his head. Foot and leg were used to support the body, hand and arm for pulling. Thus the hand became a true hand and the foot a genuine foot, opening up the possibility of the erect posture on the ground and the adaptation of the hand to higher uses. Meanwhile the climbing and leaping from branch to branch, the measuring with the eye of distances and strength of branches, the power of grasping the right point at the right instant, and all the complicated series of movements combined in this form of locomotion furnished a marvellous set of exercises not only for the muscles but for the higher centres in the cortex of the brain. Very probably gregarious life and rude play, so common among apes, was an extension course along somewhat similar lines.

Our ancestors became at home in and well adapted to arboreal life, but the adaptation was never extreme. It was rather what Jones[1] has called a "successful minimal adaptation." They used arboreal life without abusing it by over-adaptation, which would have enslaved them, and made life on the ground an impossibility when the time came for their promotion to this new and more advanced stage.

At the close of his arboreal life the ape had inherited or acquired the following assets: His vertebrate and mammalian structure had given him a large, vigorous, compact, athletic, adaptable body. The mammalian care of the young had insured their survival, but only at the expense of great strain and risk of the mother. Something at least approaching family life was already attained. Arboreal life with its gymnastic training had moulded the body, differentiated hand and foot, given the possibility of erect posture, emancipating the hand from the work of locomotion and setting it free to become a tool-fashioning and tool-using organ. The ape has keen sense-organs, an eye for distances, and other conditions; and the use of these powers has given him a brain far superior to that of any of his humbler fellows. These

[1] 19.

are full of great possibilities and opportunities, if he will only use them.

But why did our ancestor descend from his place of safety in the trees and live on the ground, exposed to the attacks of fierce, swift, and well-armed enemies? Very few of the Primates, except the rock and cliff-inhabiting baboons, ever made this great venture. There must have been some quite compelling argument to induce him to take so great a risk. The change took place probably at some time during the latter half of the Cenozoic or Tertiary period, the last great division of geological time, the Age of mammals.[1] The earliest Tertiary Epoch, the Eocene, was a time of warm and equable climate, when apes lived far north in Europe, and doubtless in Asia also. Some of these apes were of fair or large size, showing that conditions were favorable and food abundant. The next epoch, the Oligocene, was similar but somewhat cooler. The third, the Miocene, was cooler still and dryer. Palms now forsook northern Europe, being gradually driven farther and farther south. Life became more difficult, food scarcer. Apes could not longer survive in northern Europe, but had to seek a warmer, more favorable, environment farther

[1] 5.

south, for many of the fruit and food trees had
been crowded out and famine threatened.[1]
But insects and other small and toothsome animals remained on the ground, and were abundant along the shores of rivers and lakes.
There, too, were fruits and berries, roots and
tubers. There the food supply was still more
than sufficient.

Thus far we have glanced at Europe only.
But the same changes are taking place in Asia,
the cradle and home of most placental mammals, the main area of a huge zoological province
of which Europe was but a westward projection, and with which America had direct connection from time to time in the region of
Behring's Straits. Here, during late Miocene
and early Pliocene times, in the latter part of
the Cenozoic era, a dryer and somewhat harsher
climate had been accompanied by the appearance of wide plains fitted for grazing animals,
as well as stretches of forest, with all varieties
of landscape favoring great diversity as well as
abundance of mammalian life. It was, perhaps,
the golden age for most mammals, when food
was plenty, climate not too severe, and every
prospect pleased. This slow and gradual, but
fairly steady, lowering of temperature was to

[1] 6.

culminate in the Great Ice Age of the Pleistocene Epoch, so destructive to mammalian life
in the northern hemisphere.

A second climatic change, perhaps even more
important than the lowering temperature, was
the increase of aridity. Even during the Oligocene Epoch "the flora indicates a lessening
humidity and a clearer differentiation of the
seasons."[1] The great trough of the inland sea
which had stretched from the Mediterranean
to the Indian Ocean began to rise, the first uplift taking place along the Pyrenees and western
Alps. The Miocene was marked by a series of
great movements. The old inland sea was displaced, subsidence gave place to uplift, and the
greatest mountain system of the globe, including
the Alps and the Himalayas, began to grow
through vast repeated uplifts in the crust.[2]
The continents were elevated and widened.
The forest-dwelling types became restricted and
largely exterminated, and animals of the plains,
in the form of horses, rhinoceroses, and the
cloven-hoofed ruminants, expanded in numbers
and in species. This profound faunal change
implies dryer climate. There was now a lesser
area of tropic seas to give moisture to the atmosphere. The mountains were now effective

[1] 8: 20.   [2] 5: 58–60.

barriers, shutting off the moisture-bearing winds from the interior of the continents.

These changes would have been noticeable in Europe north of the Alps, but were far more so in central Asia along the northern face of the great plateau of Thibet, with its eastern and western buttresses, and its towering rampart of the Himalayas on the south, cutting off the warm moisture of the Indian Ocean. Northward of this vast plateau and westward over the far less elevated Iranian plateau and Afghanistan, forest was fast being replaced by parklands of mingled groves and glades, or by grassy plains, or even by dry steppes. Dessication, aridity of climate, was fast compelling forest and arboreal mammals to migrate or radically change their habits of life.[1]

Almost all the apes found their old environment and continued their arboreal life by migrating far southward through India or into Africa. But at the rear of the retreating host were forms from the cooler northern regions. They were hardy and vigorous, and probably larger than most of their fellows. Possibly some of them were caught in isolated decreasing areas of forest surrounded by steppe or plain. Some of them, at least, began to descend from the

[1] M: chap. V.

trees, to seek the new food supplies of riversides, glades, and thickets, and thus gradually
to become accustomed to life on the ground.
It was a very hazardous experiment; only the
most hardy and wary and the quickest in per-
ception, wit, and movement survived. Among
these were our ancestors, driven like all their
forebears by the spur of necessity into a new
mode of life under trying conditions.

They were still only apes, with long arms and
short legs, and probably scrambled mostly on
all fours. They had heavy brows, retreating
foreheads, projecting jaws, and a brutal physi-
ognomy. Of the mental life of the man who
was to be descended from them there were few
signs. They were bundles of very slight possibilities.

But let us not "despise the day of small
things." They were still far from the invisible
line between apedom and manhood. Physically
they resembled man quite closely. They had
hand and foot, and a fair-sized brain, though
they had scarcely begun to realize the possibilities of these structures.

Arboreal life could teach them little more;
continuance in that school would have meant
a very comfortable stagnation. They were now
promoted to a new school of vastly more diffi-

cult problems, greater risks and dangers, and more severe and trying discipline. They had had an excellent course of manual and sensory training; now they must continue this and add to it the use of whatever wits they had, under peril of death. Nature was still compelling them to "move on."

This descent to the ground probably was accomplished either in India or on the Iranian plateau, or somewhat farther to the northeast, somewhere in the great horseshoe of parkland which curved around the western buttress of the great central Asiatic plateau of Thibet. Can we locate it somewhat more definitely? [1]

At this time, during the Pliocene Epoch, there were being deposited in India the so-called Siwalik strata — vast, ancient flood-plains, stretching for a distance of 1,500 miles along the southern foot-hills of the Himalayas. They are composed of materials washed down from the mountains by a system of rivers, persisting with little change into the present. Says Osborn of the mammals found here: "It is altogether the grandest assemblage of mammals the world has ever seen, distributed through southern and eastern Asia, and probably, if our vision could be extended, ranging westward toward Persia and

[1] 1: 671.

Arabia into northern Africa. It is the most truly cosmopolitan aggregation because in its Upper Pliocene stage it represents a congress of mammals from four great continents. . . . The only continents which do not contribute to this assemblage are South America and Australia."[1] The older, Miocene, portions of this fauna are chiefly browsing forest forms, emphasized by the absence of both horses and Hipparion, as well as of grazing types of cattle and antelopes. Grazing forms, showing the decline of the forest and the spread of open parkland and grassy areas, become abundant during the Pliocene Epoch. "Among the Primates we find the Orang, an ape now confined to Borneo and Sumatra; also the Chimpanzee, another ape, now confined to Africa, the Siwalik species displaying a more human type of dentition than that of the existing African form."

In the older, Miocene, portion we find Sivapithecus, an ape which Pilgrim considers as more nearly resembling man than any other genus of anthropoids, while Gregory speaks of it as belonging to the anthropoid line.[2] Somewhat later, in late Pliocene or early Pleistocene, there was living not far away, in Java, a far more renowned form, *Pithecanthropus erectus, Du*

---

[1] 5: 321, 327, 275. [2] 7, 10.

Bois, which seems to stand almost exactly midway between higher apes and man. The remains consisted of two molar teeth, a thigh-bone, and the top of a skull. The cranium is low, the forehead exceedingly retreating, giving but very small space for the frontal lobes of the brain. But the brain-cast, made from the cranial cavity, shows, according to Du Bois, that the speech area is about twice as large as in certain apes, though only one-half as large as in man. In size the brain stands somewhat above midway between the highest recent apes and the lowest existing men. The thigh-bone shows that Pithecanthropus could have stood and walked erect quite comfortably. There has been and still is much difference of opinion regarding the position of this most interesting being. Opinion was long divided nearly equally between those who considered it as the highest ape and others who held it to be the very lowest man.

It is worthy of notice that, when Pithecanthropus was alive, "Java was a part of the Asiatic continent; and similar herds of great mammals roamed freely over the plains from the foot-hills of the Himalaya Mountains to the borders of the ancient Trinil River, while similar apes inhabited the forests. At the same

time the Orang may have entered the forests
of Borneo, which are at present its home."[1]
Where man's distant cousins, the anthropoid
apes, and his still nearer relation, Pithecanthropus, were all living and some, at least, apparently progressing, could hardly have been
far from his original home. But the climatic
conditions of that time lead us to seek his original cradle somewhat farther northward than
India, or even Beluchistan, and nearer to, if
not in, the great steppe zone of central Asia.
We lose sight of our ape-man as he is advancing
toward the threshold of manhood, not far away.
Whether we think that Pithecanthropus was approaching or had already passed it depends
much upon where we draw the line between
ape and man, a line largely artificial and as
difficult to fix as the day and hour when the
youth becomes of age, and what human characteristics we select to mark it. In his erect
posture and some other physical traits he seems
already to have attained manhood; mentally
he was probably far inferior to even the lowest savage races of to-day. We are not sure
whether he was our ancestor or merely a cousin
of our ancestor, once or twice removed; we still
lack foundations for any hypotheses as to ex-

[1] 24–26.

actly when, where, or how the erect ancestral
ape-man emerged into real manhood.

Millennia passed between the days of Pithecanthropus and the first human migrations, and
we may imagine primitive man as having become fairly well accustomed to life on the
ground, and as having mastered his first lessons in meeting its dangers and difficulties. He
had probably taken possession of a much wider
area than the home of the ape-man, perhaps of
the whole of the parkland zone curving around
the western buttresses of the plateau of Thibet.
From this region routes of migration radiated
in all directions, all the more open because of the
elevation of land which lasted through Upper
Pliocene and early Pleistocene times.[1]   Sumatra
and Java then formed an extension of the Malay
Peninsula, reaching more than 1,000 miles into
the Indian Ocean; while the Orang seems to
have been able to reach Borneo somewhat
earlier. The way was equally clear westward
into Europe, the Dardanelles being then replaced by a land bridge, while a second bridge
spanned the Mediterranean over Sicily into
Italy, and a third existed at Gibraltar.[2]   These
routes were evidently followed by herds of great

[1] 5: 373.   [2] 40: 35.

herbivora, and probably by the earliest human emigrants into Europe.

Following Keane,[1] we shall divide mankind into four great groups or races, and then glance at their radiation from southwestern Asia toward all parts of the globe. These great primitive divisions are:

I. *Negroids.* Color yellowish brown to black, stature large or very small. Hair short, black or reddish brown, frizzly, flattened-elliptical in cross-section. Nose broad and flattened. Cheek-bones small, somewhat retreating. Examples: Negritoes, Negroes.

II. *Mongoloids.* Color yellowish. Stature below average. Hair coarse, lank, round in cross-section. Nose very small. Cheek-bones prominent. Examples: Malays, Chinese, Japanese, Thibetans, Siberian "Hyperboreans."

III. *Americans.* Color reddish or coppery. Stature large. Hair long, lank, coarse, black, round in cross-section. Nose large, bridged, or aquiline. Cheek-bones moderately prominent. (Probably a branch of II.) Examples: Indians of North and South America.

IV. *Caucasians.* Color pale or florid. Hair long, wavy or straight, elliptical in cross-section. Nose large, straight or arched. Cheek-bones

[1] **30**: 228.

small, unmarked. Examples: Hamitic, Semitic, and European peoples.

We may now imagine quite primitive human beings starting from their early home and seeking their fortunes widely apart. They came under quite different climatic and other physical conditions. Their environment, problems, stimuli, and opportunities were unlike. Thus, having become more or less unlike in the homeland, they gradually became differentiated into the present great groups or races already mentioned. Some started earlier or marched more rapidly than others. Many proved unequal to the dangers and difficulties of the journey or new place of settlement, and disappeared. Many stagnated or degenerated. Only the comparatively successful or fortunate have survived. Hence, our scheme is hardly an adequate expression of prehistoric racial groups and their characteristics, except in very general outline.

We have seen that the apes, retreating before the approach of harsh and dry climatic conditions and diminished forest areas and food supply, migrated southward into India and Africa. The Orang settled in Borneo, Pithecanthropus in Java, the Chimpanzee and Gorilla went into Africa. These routes presented the fewest difficulties and demanded the least readaptation or change of habit. The climate was mild and food generally abundant and easily obtained. Their environment was neither stimulating, trying, nor exacting. Progress was hardly to be expected, but survival was far easier than in more northerly regions.

The Negritos followed almost exactly the same routes. We find them purest and perhaps least modified in the "Pygmies" of the African forests; but also in the Malay Peninsula, the Andaman Islands, and the Philippines. De Morgan believes that he has found proofs of their presence on the Iranian plateau at a comparatively late date.

Behind them Negroid peoples poured into Africa, apparently in successive waves. Some of them went into the Malay Peninsula, probably generally submerging the Negritos, and reached New Guinea and Australia. Inhabiting a series of islands and other more or less isolated areas, mingling often with Negritos, probably later also more or less with the Malays, they became much modified, and their relations to the African Negroes and to one another are still anything but clear.

The Mongoloids pushed eastward. The earliest migrations seem to be those of the Malays, a great, very interesting, and little-known though

much-studied group of peoples. They followed
the oceanic Negritos along the Malay Peninsula
and occupied the great chains of islands stretching through the Indian Ocean and far into the
Pacific, through more than ninety degrees of
longitude along the equator. But much of this
spread is probably of quite recent date.

The Mongoloid peoples seem to have passed
along the northern front of the Central Asiatic
plateau into Siberia, China, and Japan, and to
have sent off the great American branch. Even
before the Mongols had started on their eastward journey the Caucasians may have turned
westward, following the old Negroid route.
There was probably also more or less of an eastern dispersal, but we cannot consider the problem of these Oriental Caucasic remnants and
traces. The great body went westward. The
Hamitic peoples distributed themselves along
the southern shore of the Mediterranean, and
many may well have occupied a large part of the
Sahara region, then a land of water-courses
capable of supporting a large population. Behind them came the Semitic folk. Judging from
their languages the Hamitic and Semitic peoples seem to have been in contact over a wide
area, and for a long space of time. The
Semites found a new and permanent home in

Arabia, on whose plateaus and surrounding grass-lands they increased and multiplied, and sent off fresh waves of migration and conquest in all directions.

We have already noticed that our classification of races is based upon a study of recent and still surviving peoples. The very earliest inhabitants of Europe would find no place in it. Probably they long antedated the Hamites. African Negroids and Caucasians came from a common home, and journeyed for a time over a common road, though probably at far different times. It would be strange if the earliest inhabitants of Europe showed no traces of this common home and ancestry. Since the remote period which we are considering Negroes and Caucasians have become widely different, and their racial characters have become clear and sharp. This may not have been altogether the case with the first peoples to arrive in Europe. But attempts to relate the Neanderthal crania with those of modern Australians or Tasmanians, or any existing race, have met with no great success. In regard to these questions we are still in the dark.

Beside the African routes into Europe, along the south shore of the Mediterranean and over the Sicilian and Gibraltar land bridges, while they lasted, two others must be noticed. One of these extended through Asia Minor and across the land bridge at the Dardanelles, while the second led westward along the northern border of the Caspian and Black Seas and the Caucasus Mountains. The most southerly of these four routes through Africa were probably the first to be travelled, the most northerly last of all. We shall have to study these routes more closely in a later chapter.

It was at some time during the Glacial period, the Great Ice Age, when a vast ice-cap covered northern Europe with glaciers extending far southward and advancing or retreating according to climatic conditions, that man arrived in Europe. During the first Glacial Epoch the advance of the ice covered the most northern part of Great Britain and the Rhine valley almost as far south as Cologne; Scandinavia was completely buried, like central Greenland to-day, and North Germany probably to the Harz Mountains. Eastward the southern edge of the ice sheet ran nearly along the line of 50° N. lat. across Russia. In Siberia the effects were less marked and the limits were much farther northward. Between the parallel of 50° and the northern edge of the Alpine glaciers a zone was left ice-free, but three-fifths of Germany was overwhelmed. Southern England and France, not yet separated by the English Channel, formed one great habitable province, and but a small part of France was glaciated. The climate was tempered by proximity to the sea.[1] The average yearly temperature of northern Europe was probably not more than 4°–6° Cent. (39°–43° Fahr.), which is colder than at present. But the formation of these enormous masses of ice demanded heavy snowfall and a moist or very damp climate. Hence the edge of the great ice sheet advanced or retreated according to climatic conditions.

There were four periods of advance before the final retreat of the ice, not counting minor oscillations.[2] These are known as the Gunz, Mindel, Riss, and Wurm Glacial Epochs. Alternating with these were the interglacial epochs of ice retreat — the Gunz-Mindel, Mindel-Riss, and Riss-Wurm; while the final retreat is usually termed post-glacial. During the first and second interglacial epochs the climate appears to have been warmer than at present. But at times dryness may have contributed to the retreat of the ice even more than warmth,

[1] **40**: chap. II.   **D**: I, 17–110.
[2] For maps showing extent of ice at different glacial epochs, see **41**: vol. II, p. 419.   **42**: end of volume.

and then the climate would have been continental, harsh, and extreme.

Even during epochs of glacial advance conditions in France and in the German zone must have been better than we should expect. Some kind of grazing or browsing pasturage must have been rich and abundant to support large animals like the reindeer or even the woolly mammoths characteristic of the second and third glacial epochs, which furnished abundant food for prehistoric hunters. Farther south the glacial epochs may well have been times of heavy rainfall, transforming the Sahara desert and the dryer steppes and plateaus of Asia into veritable gardens.

The retreating ice left behind it a land covered with rocks, clays, gravels, and sands brought by the glaciers and their streams. Here and there basins had been gouged out where lakes or ponds long remained — as in Maine and Minnesota to-day — to be later drained, or, if shallow, to be overgrown with sphagnum and changed into great bogs. Scattered thickets of shrubs and stunted hardy trees, poplars, willows, and others occurred. In sheltered and well-drained valleys and mountainsides the trees grew larger and even forests began to appear. This tundra landscape still characterizes wide areas of northern Canada and Siberia.[1]

The tundra was followed by steppe conditions, where elevation of land to the north and northwest had cut off the tempering oceanic winds. The climate was harsh, dry, continental, with cold winters and hot summers. The winds carried great storms of dust and piled it up in drifts in valleys and on suitably situated mountainsides in the form of loess, so important to the future agricultural development of Europe, though its most massive accumulation is seen in China, which received and held the driftings from the great elevated plains of central Asia. As the climate became moister, if the temperature did not fall too low, steppe finally gave way to the meadow and forest of modern Europe. Tundra, steppe, and forest had each its special types of animal as well as plant life. The characteristic tundra animal is the reindeer, though musk-ox, woolly mammoth, and others were wide-spread at this time. The peculiar steppe animal is the horse. The characteristic forest and meadow animals are the deer and their allies; the wolf and bear; the wild boar and cattle seem to be at home in forest and glade and along the streams.

[1] See Charts, 40: 41–43. 5. Also 40: 45, 46; 412–427; 386.

In France, where there was far less glacia-
tion, the succession of tundra, steppe, and forest
is less apparent. Here we find a mingling of
varied forms which have come in from very
different regions, driven from their original
homes by change of climate or drawn by favorable conditions.

The first unmistakable relic of man in Europe
is a human lower jaw found in the Mauer sands
near Heidelberg, some seventy-nine feet below
the surface of the bluff.[1] It seems to belong to
the second or Mindel-Riss interglacial epoch,
and its age is estimated by Osborn at about
250,000 years. Remains characteristic of the
oldest Paleolithic epochs occur between thirty
and forty-five feet below the surface. If we are
to find an archæological name for this epoch,
there seems to be no better one than Eolithic,
the dawn of the Stone Age, when European man
had hardly more than begun to chip a stone implement, although we must recognize the un-
readiness of many or most archæologists to find
a place for such rude products.[2]

The third interglacial period (Riss-Wurm) and
the fourth period of advance (Wurm) cover
what is known as Lower Paleolithic time, which
is the earlier four-fifths or more of the Old Stone

[1] 40: 95. 47.   [2] D: I, 380–412. 48.

Age or Paleolithic period, extending approximately from 125,000 B. C., to 25,000 B. C. During the greater part of this period Europe was occupied by the Neanderthaloid people. Neanderthal man had a very large head with heavy, overhanging eyebrows meeting above the nose, and a markedly retreating forehead. The face was high and the large nasal opening indicates a broad, flat nose. The lower jaw was heavy and the chin retreating. The trunk was short, thick, and robust, the shoulders broad; the limbs short and heavy, the arms and lower legs relatively short, and the hands very large. Although the much-discussed Piltdown skull may quite probably be regarded as belonging to the earliest part of this period, the finer form of cranium seems to testify to a higher race of better mental development than the Neanderthaloids, huddling in their caves and shelters. It may easily represent a far more progressive ancestral race, of which they are somewhat degenerate descendants, though Osborn dissents from this view.[1]

Their remains are found in caves and rock-shelters all over Europe. Here we find their hearths; the bones of the animals which they had hunted for their food; their almond-shaped

[1] 40: 130, 244.

flint axes, "hand-stones" (*Coups-de-Poing*), the scrapers for dressing skins and shaving wooden tools, and a variety of other forms. Here they buried their dead. During the third warm interglacial epoch they lived in the open, as at the station of Chelles, which has given its name to the earliest Paleolithic epoch.[1] Their origin and route of migration is quite uncertain, but it seems probable that they entered Europe from the southern shore of the Mediterranean.

The post-glacial period is characterized by the final retreat of the ice. The change of climate was not steady but marked by a series of oscillations, repeating on a much smaller scale the glacial and interglacial epochs of the long past. The climatic change is accompanied by the appearance of tundra and steppe, followed by meadows and the forest conditions of modern times. Game was abundant and general conditions severe but healthy and fairly favorable.

A new race has appeared on the scene which replaced the Neanderthal folk, and had practically none of their primitive or degenerate, ape-like characteristics.[2] The Cro-Magnon people have excited the wonder and admiration of all anthropologists. They were of tall stature,

[1] D: I, 113.   [2] 40: 290, 316.

had long legs, especially below the knee, giving swiftness in running. The forehead is broad and of good height, the features are rugged but attractive, and the brain is very large. They seem to represent a new race and new immigration, probably from Asia, which spread over Europe.

The Cro-Magnon brain was anything but dull. In this remote time, more than 20,000 years ago, there sprang up an art never since surpassed in its own field except, perhaps, by that of the Greeks. Their bone implements are adorned with the most lifelike carvings or sculptures. On the walls of caves we find paintings as realistic and alive, and often as finely executed in detail and coloring, as the best animal painters of our day could produce. These people must have had a high and keen appreciation of the beauty of form and proportion. All this artistic movement must have had its source in new ideas and conditions, springing from a thinking as well as a feeling and observing mind. They also frequently buried their dead, decorated with strings of perforated shells, and surrounded by flints or sometimes by a layer of red earth or ore. With them were the bones of food animals and the flint weapons needed for the journey into or use in the life beyond.

The life of the Cro-Magnon hunters on their arrival in Europe was anything but unendurable, especially along the Riviera. There were open-air encampments where men passed at least the summer months in tents or huts. The race seems to have culminated during the cold middle Magdalenian epoch, which indicates that they were well adapted to its conditions. Game was abundant and relatively easily captured. They had food and raiment, fair shelter, excellent art, alert brains, and probably a fair degree of social life. They may well have been content, courageous, and full of hope for themselves and their descendants.

Upper Paleolithic time, beginning with the arrival of the Cro-Magnons, about 25,000 years ago, is divided into four epochs, or, better, four culture-stages: Aurignacian, Solutrean, Magdalenian, and Azilian-Tardenoisian. Even in late Magdalenian days, after a cold and dry interval accompanied by steppe conditions and a new formation of loess, the air became moister and the temperature gradually moderated until it became much like that of to-day. Tundra and steppe animals became more rare; a forest and meadow fauna took possession of Europe. Instead of the reindeer we find stag and roe-deer, cattle, wild boar, bears and wolves, beaver and otter. These were less easily hunted and prob-

HUMAN FIGURES, SPAIN—EARLY NEOLITHIC

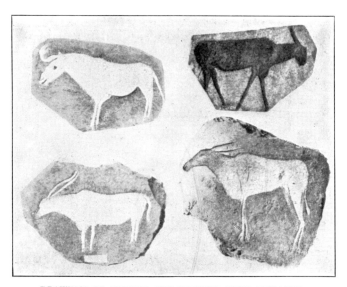

DRAWINGS OF ANIMALS (CRO-MAGNON) FROM ALTAMIRA

ably less abundant than the reindeer and horse
had been.   As hunting became less profitable,
fishing grew more attractive.   The streams probably swarmed with fish, and the salmon was
probably as abundant throughout northern
Europe as in Scandinavia to-day.   A change of
life is suggested by the implements.   The harpoons became ruder.   The beautifully flaked
lance-heads and the smoothed bone daggers give
place to small flints, "microliths," less fitted for
attacking large and dangerous animals.   The
country seems to have supported a smaller and
decreasing population.   Cro-Magnon man had
always been a reindeer hunter, accustomed and
well adapted to the life and conditions of tundra or steppe.   The changes were not in his
favor or to his liking.   Many probably left
France and Germany.   Those who remained
deserted the rock-shelters and cave-mouths,
where every spring the water seeping down and
dripping through the roof dislodged masses of
stone.[1]   The shelter was less needed.   Men
dwelt more in the open, and fewer records of
their presence were preserved.

But Europe was not deserted.   There was no
"hiatus."   Other peoples were coming in, perhaps better suited to the new conditions, probably mostly of Asiatic origin.   Broad-heads, as

[1] E: 110–117.

well as new long-heads, appear, less attractive physically and mentally, but apparently of tougher fibre and greater staying power than our more striking and charming Cro-Magnons.[1]   A new grand mingling of peoples had already begun or was in its last stages of preparation already advancing from afar in successive waves. In Italy genuine Neolithic culture may already have been introduced.   It steals very slowly into northern Europe and overspreads it.   The Cro-Magnon race generally migrated or died out, but left its traces in the physical characters of the people of Dordogne and elsewhere.

The Azilian-Tardenoisian epoch leads over to the Neolithic, our chief object of study.   Its relative position in prehistoric time is shown in the following scheme:

A. Eolithic Period.   Stone implements exceedingly rude, hardly recognizable as artificially chipped; otherwise like *B.*

B. Paleolithic Period.   Stone implements chipped or flaked, never polished.   No domesticated plants or animals.   No pottery.   Man a collector or hunter, more rarely a fisherman.

C.   Transition Period, resembling *B* in most respects.

[*A, B,* and *C* make up the Old Stone Age, before the use of metals.]

[1] 40: 475-500.

D. *Neolithic Period.* Some stone implements polished. No metal except that copper is introduced toward the end of the period. Agriculture with domestic plants and animals. Pottery but no potter's wheel. Dawn of Civilization.

E. *Bronze Period.* Bronze implements or utensils. Dawn of History. Begins about 2500 B. C. in northern Europe.

F. *Iron Period.* Iron introduced. Historic Times. Begins about 1000 B. C. in northern Europe.

CHAPTER II

THE PERIOD OF TRANSITION. SHELL–HEAPS

DURING the last great advance of the ice in the earlier Magdalenian epoch the Scandinavian peninsula had been buried beneath a great mass of ice, and resembled the central portion of Greenland to-day. A great glacier extended southward, obliterating the Baltic Sea and crowding into northern Germany. As the glaciers withdrew, North Germany became a vast tundra, across which we may imagine the reindeer and other Arctic and subarctic mammals retreating northeastward before the milder forest and meadow conditions already prevailing in France and Russia.[1] The low temperature of the water of the emerging Baltic is shown by the presence of an arctic bivalve, *Yoldia arctica*, which has given its name to the epoch. A few scattered bone implements show the presence of reindeer hunters in Germany at this time.

Before the close of the Yoldia period Germany began to pass from tundra to forest — a transformation which was also now progressing in Denmark. The temperature moderated slowly.

---

[1] D: 466, 476; 40: 281.

The land rose in such a way that it separated the Baltic from the North Sea and the Arctic Ocean, with which it had been connected, and made of it a great fresh-water lake. The characteristic animal of this lake was a small pond animal, *ancylus*, which has given its name to both lake and epoch.

The next epoch — the Litorina (or Tapes) depression — was characterized by a sinking of the land in which the barrier between the Baltic and the North Seas gave place to a wide communication. The Baltic became more salt than at present, and the oyster-banks became abundant. It was during this epoch that the shell-heaps were accumulated.

The following chart gives a condensed view of the succession of events (in reverse order):[1]

WESTERN AND MIDDLE EUROPE	NORTHERN EUROPE	DATE B. C.
4. Typical Neolithic.	Typical Neolithic. Beech and fir forests.	6000– 2500
3. Daun Stage.	Litorina Epoch. Oak forests. Northern climatic optimum.	8000
Campignian.	Shell-heaps.	
2. Gschnitz Stage.	Ancylus Epoch. Birch and pine forests.	10,000
Azilian-Tardenoisian.	Magelmose.	
1. Bühl Stage.	Yoldia Epoch. Swedish-Finnish Moraines.	16,000
Magdalenian (later).	Tundra. Dryas Flora.	

[1] D: 466, 476; 40: 281.

The growth and succession of the forests of Denmark, accompanying changes in conditions of soil and climate, have been clearly traced by Steenstrup.[1] The scene of his investigations was a moraine country broken by low ranges of hills in the island of Zealand, north of Copenhagen. The hills are often strewn with erratic blocks of rock brought by glaciers, with here and there small lakes, ponds, or peat-bogs often giving place to meadow or forest.

Some of these depressions are filled with a poor variety of peat, dug for fuel, and the sides are often abrupt, steep, and deep. These sides furnish a calendar by showing the different layers which have been formed by successive generations of tree-growth falling into the bog. Thus, in the upper layers we find remains of trees which still flourish in Denmark, while the deepest strata contain the remains of reindeer. The thickness of these layers is between five and seven metres. Their formation, according to Steenstrup, occupied 10,000 to 12,000 years.[1]

The following layers are found in these "calendars," beginning at the surface:

1. Surface layer. Remains of the beech, which furnishes the chief beauty of the forests of Denmark to-day.

[1] C: 225; 60.

2. Oak. The beginning of this layer was contemporary with the Litorina depression.

3. Scotch pine (*pinus sylvestris*). The earliest pines were dwarfed, the trunks showing as many as seventy rings to the inch. In upper strata their trunks were a metre or so in diameter. In the Lillemose moor, near Rudesdal, the whole eastern side, twenty metres deep, was filled with pines. While no human remains have been found in these moors, a stone axe embedded in a pine trunk, and a stone arrow-head in a bone of the *bos primigenius* (which, like the auerhahn or pine partridge lived on the young pine shoots) have been discovered. The soil best adapted to the pine is a damp soil, poor in humus, whereas the present rich, fertile soil of Denmark is best suited to the beech. This explains the fact that pine forests no longer grow there.

4. At the bottom, poplars and aspens. The clay underlying the pines and poplars contains leaves of arctic willows and saxifrages.

Through these types of strata we may trace the epochs described at the beginning of the chapter. The pine characterizes the Azilian-Tardenoisian-Ancylus Epoch; at the time of the Litorina depression it was fast giving place to the oak, which remains characteristic of the Neolithic and Bronze periods, yielding to the beech during the Iron Age. But this advance must have been gradual and the boundary of advance irregular.

Blytt has traced a very similar succession of changes in flora and climate in southern Norway, and Geikie in Scotland.[1] These changes are very important in our study of the traces of man's first appearance in Denmark as furnishing not only their setting but also their chronology.

Shell-heaps are found all over the world in favorable sheltered localities where sea food is abundant, especially near clam flats. Hence they are not characteristic of any one race or time. Some are very ancient, some comparatively or very modern. They merely show the remains of the camping-grounds of people in a low stage of culture. Every one has its own history and its own slight or marked peculiarities.

The Danish shell-heaps or kitchen-middens are mounds generally about fifty metres wide and one hundred metres long, and perhaps one metre in thickness. But, as we should naturally expect, the size varies greatly according to the advantages of the situation, the number of inhabitants, and the length of time that it was inhabited.

[1] 42: 270.

SHELL–HEAP

SHELL–HEAP AXE

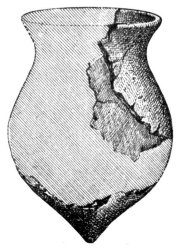

SHELL–HEAP JAR

The age of these shell-heaps is shown approximately by the presence of the auerhahn, proving the neighborhood of pine forests. The charcoal in the fireplaces came from oak wood, showing that oak forests are overspreading the country. The Baltic was more salt than at present, and the shore line was depressed. These facts indicate a period of transition from the Ancylus to the Litorina Epoch. The stone implements resemble those of western Europe during the late transition epoch, and do not occur in the oldest graves. There are no domestic animals except the dog, and no cultivated plants except some wheat in the later remains. All this seems to prove that genuine Neolithic culture had not yet reached the shores of the Baltic. They are composed mostly of oyster shells with a mingling of those of scallops, mussels, and periwinkles. The oyster has now disappeared from large parts of the coast and in others has decreased in size. Land elevation has narrowed the connection of the Baltic with the North Sea, and the water contains less salt.

Remains of cod and herring show that the fishermen who lived on or near these harbors ventured out to sea in dugouts or on rafts, and that they must have made lines for fishing in fairly deep water. Remains of other fish occur. Bones of birds are often very abundant, especially swamp, shore, and swimming species; wild geese and ducks, swans and gulls, the *Alca impennis* or wingless auk, now extinct. The blackcock, or "spruce (pine) partridge," was then common, but has now disappeared from Denmark with the pine whose buds formed a large part of its food.

Bones of stag, deer, and wild boar form, according to Steenstrup, 97 per cent of all those of mammals found at Havelse.[1] Bones of seal, otter, wolf, fox, bear, beaver, and wildcat also occur. There are no traces of reindeer or musk-ox. These animals had already migrated or died out. Steenstrup noticed that the long bones of birds are about twenty times as numerous as others of their skeletons, and that the heads or ends of the long bones of mammals are generally missing. These were exactly the parts which are gnawed by dogs, whose remains also occur. Hence he drew the inference, now universally accepted, that the dog was domesticated in Denmark at this time. It was a small species, apparently akin to the jackal and of southeastern origin. No remains of other domesticated animals have been found, nor of cultivated plants, except a few casts of grains

[1] L: 235.

of wheat in the pottery of the upper layers of some of the heaps.

Daggers, awls, and needles were made of bone; also combs apparently used for stretching sinews into long threads. The flint implements are rudely chipped, never polished. We find long flakes used as knives, and numerous scrapers and borers.[1] The axe, if we may call it so, was of peculiar form, approaching the triangular and looking as if made out of a circular disk of flint by breaking away two sides of the periphery, leaving a somewhat flaring cutting edge. The middle was thick, the edge tapered somewhat rapidly, making a rough but quite durable instrument. Longer implements in the form of chisels or picks were also roughly flaked with skilfully retouched edges, often with one end narrowed or bluntly pointed. In all cases the work is very rude compared with the best specimens of Paleolithic time. Arrow-heads are common, usually with a broad edge instead of a point, well suited to killing birds and small mammals. The bone harpoon seems to have gone out of use.

The pottery is thick, heavy, crude, with practically no ornament, except finger-prints around the upper edge. The jars are sometimes of

[1] A: 329.

large size; often the base is pointed instead of flat or rounded. Hearths of calcined stones are abundant. Sometimes these are surrounded by circular depressions in the heaps, which may mark the form and position of huts or shelters; or these may have been placed under the lee of the near-by forests. No graves or human remains of this period have been found.

Shell-heaps quite similar to those of Denmark were discovered at Mugem, in Portugal, in the valley of the Tagus, twenty-five to thirty metres above sea-level, and thirty to forty miles from the mouth of the river. The shells are of marine origin, and indicate a considerable elevation of land since their accumulation. The stone implements are very primitive and of Azilian-Tardenoisian type. Large flat stones, perhaps for grinding, perhaps for dressing skins, occur. Pottery occurs only in the upper layers, where the bones of mammals increase in number. There are no polished implements, no traces of domesticated animals, not even of the tame dog. Graves were found here and there; and while the skulls were badly contorted, they seemed to show that the inhabitants were partly long-headed, partly broad-heads. Remains, apparently of the same age, have been found in Great Britain.

Even the Danish shell-heaps are not all of the same age. According to Forrer, Havno is ancient; Ertebolle is also old, but was long inhabited, and some of its uppermost layers may be full Neolithic; Aalborg and others are younger. Mugem strikes us as more ancient than the similar Danish remains. Other remains near the Baltic suggest very strongly quite marked differences in age or in the culture of their inhabitants, or in both these respects. We can notice only two of these.

Maglemose lies on the west coast of Zealand near the harbor of Mullerup. Here a peat-bog has encroached upon a fresh-water lake and has covered a mud bottom strewn with shells of pond-snails and mussels. Pines had grown in the swamp, and their stumps still protrude into or above the moss. The implements were found a little above the old lake bottom between seventy centimetres and one metre below the surface of the peat. The remains of the settlement were distributed over an area about one hundred feet long and broad. The charred or burned wood was very largely (eighty per cent) pine, ten per cent hazel, a little elm and poplar. No oak was found here, but oak-pollen grains were found in the same level as the settlement, or slightly higher and later. Flint cracked by heat and charred fragments of wood were found, but no definite hearths. Bones of fresh-water fish and of swamp turtles occur. The shore could not have been very distant even if it stood considerably higher, but no bones of marine fish have been found. Many birds were hunted. The mammals include boar, deer, stag, and urus. The dog is the only domesticated animal.

Flint chips are abundant at Maglemose; long knife-flakes and axes are rare. Scrapers and nuclei are numerous. The arrow-heads are long and pointed instead of broad and edged, as in the usual Danish shell-heap. Many of these so-called arrow-heads may have been nothing more than microliths used for a great variety of purposes. No flint implements or fragments show any trace of polishing. Bone implements are numerous. We find rude harpoons of a very late Magdalenian type. Also, some of the bone implements are ornamented with various patterns of incised lines, and even one or two rude drawings of animals occur. The culture evidently differs quite markedly from that of the ordinary shell-heaps. It is worthy of notice that the mud of the lake bottom and the overlying peat were continuous over and around the whole area of the settlement; there is no sign of any island at this point and the settlement was some 350 metres from the original shore of the lake. There are abundant traces of fire but no hearths. No traces of piles have been discovered. All this seems to corroborate Sarauw's view that the people lived on a raft all the year round. Sarauw considers the remains as of the same age as the oldest shell-heaps. But there is a wide-spread tendency to consider Maglemose as considerably older, belonging probably to the close of the Ancylus Epoch.

Virchow has described a heap composed of mussel-shells on the outlet of Burtnecker Lake, east of Riga, called Rinnekalns.[1] Its most interesting feature is its pottery made of clay mixed with powdered mussel-shells, giving it a peculiar glitter. It is ornamented with lines arranged in an angular geometrical pattern encircling the vessel. Similar pottery can be followed far southward into Russia and westward as far as East Prussia, but not farther into Germany. Bored teeth used for ornaments occur. Bone implements are numerous, often ornamented with fine lines in zigzag or network. We find harpoons also. The flint industry was poorly and sparingly developed. Graves were discovered, but their contents proved that they belonged to a much later period.

[1] 63.

The culture is peculiar, paralleled to a certain extent but not repeated in western Europe. We still seem to detect the influence of a decadent, late Magdalenian style of ornament. Virchow considered them as very late Paleolithic or very early Neolithic.

The shell-heaps of different regions resemble one another in general features, but differ and show their individuality in details of culture. These peculiarities may be due to difference of age or of culture or population, or to both. We must first attempt to find some place for them in the chronological succession discovered in France. They cannot be much older than the French period of transition, when Scandinavia first became habitable. But good cave-series covering the transition epoch are rare, and usually very incomplete. In 1887 Piette found a remarkable series in a cave or natural tunnel at Mas d'Azil, near Toulouse.[1] The most important strata were the following:

1. A dark layer evidently Magdalenian.

2. A yellow layer deposited by river floods.

3. Dark Magdalenian layer, with reindeer harpoons, engravings, and sculptures. Reindeer becoming rare; stag increasing.

4. Barren yellow layer, like 2.

[1] **40**: 459; **A**: I, 314; **D**: 213.

5. Reddish layer (Azilian). No reindeer. Stag abundant. Flints nearly all of Magdalenian types. Flattened stag-horn harpoons perforated at base. Bone points and smoothers. Pointed flat pebbles. Bones of stag, bear, boar, wildcat, beaver.

6. Bones of wild boar, stag, horse. Flints similar to those in 5. Beginnings of pottery and of polishing; but not of polished axes. Piette's Arisian. Beginning of Neolithic.

7. Neolithic and Bronze remains.

Layer 5 evidently represents a period posterior to the Magdalenian and anterior to the real Neolithic. Hence Piette considered it as marking a distinct Azilian Epoch, resembling the Magdalenian in most of its flint implements, in the absence of pottery and of polished axes. But the reindeer has here given place to the stag, and the harpoon has changed correspondingly and is less skilfully made. Bone implements are decadent.

Another culture, the Tardenoisian, was of exceedingly wide range. It took its name from Fère-en-Tardenois, Department of Aisne, northeast of Paris, and was characterized by its very small "pygmy" flints of various, usually geometric forms.[1] This microlithic industry was

[1] **40**: 465.

found in France, Belgium, England, Germany, Russia, and along the southern shore of the Mediterranean. The culture was well represented along rivers and inlets, and seemed to characterize a fishing rather than hunting folk.

In 1909 Breuil and Obermaier found in the grotto of Valle, in northern Spain, a classic Azilian deposit, forming the lower levels of a series rich in these microliths or pygmy flints. The Azilian was more nearly a continuation of the Magdalenian culture, while the Tardenoisian, in France, seemed to be an importation from the Mediterranean region. Since the two were so closely related in point of time it seemed safe and wise to combine the two names and call the epoch the Azilian-Tardenoisian, the Azilian representing the older portion.

The station of Campigny, on the lower Seine, seems to be somewhat later than the Azilian-Tardenoisian.[1] Here, in a pit oval in outline, with a long diameter of 4.30 metres, evidently an ancient dwelling, there were found bits of pottery, utensils of older stone epochs, no polished implements, but the tranchet or axe and the pick (pic) characteristic of the Danish shell-heaps. These Campignian remains are hardly

[1] A: I, 326.

widely enough diffused or sufficiently definite to give name to a distinct epoch. They may well be nearly contemporaneous with the (older?) shell-heaps.

The whole transition epoch, which we have hastily surveyed, shows us a series or mixture of disconnected cultures, yet with curious and striking interrelations. This may be partly due to the fact that the population of Europe was diminished and scattered. Little groups of people formed more or less isolated communities, and developed their own special peculiarities according to situation, needs, and opportunities. Connecting links, or intermediate cultures, which may once have existed, have been completely lost or still remain to be discovered. The general desertion of the caves destroyed one of our best sources of continuous records.

But the cause of this diversity lies deeper. New cultures and new waves of migration of peoples were pouring into Europe, especially into the Baltic region now left free of ice, enjoying a mild climate, and offering an abundance of food along the shores of its rivers, lakes, and seas. The Tardenoisian culture had spread northward from the Mediterranean. The broad-headed people of Furfooz, Grenelle, and Ofret had apparently crossed Europe from the east and had settled in a long zone extending northward and southward through Belgium and France and probably southward into Spain, for we remember the broad-heads found at Mugem, in Portugal. But their distribution was far wider than this strip of territory. New Neolithic types of culture had already entered Italy, perhaps as early as Magdalenian times. Series of waves appear to have passed into Poland, Russia, and Siberia, and to have moved northward until they reached the coast in Scandinavia and to the eastward. In all these cases we may probably imagine a gradual and perhaps slow infiltration or "seeping" in of the new population rather than an invasion in crowds or masses, such as we are likely to imagine. Vast stretches of habitable land had been newly opened, and there was plenty of room for all comers. In many regions the old population may have remained comparatively undisturbed until a much later date. But even they slowly came under the influence of the new and improved technique and mode of life. All this collision of culture and conflict of peoples meant stimuli, awakening, the jogging of dull minds, a veritable spur of necessity. A new day was beginning to break. The dawn was dim and cloudy, but there was the possibility and prospect of clear shining.

CHAPTER III

LAND HABITATIONS

OUR history of Paleolithic times is drawn very largely from the successive strata of remains found in rock-shelters and near the mouths of caves, where the succession of epochs is clear and indubitable. We naturally look for similar reliable testimony concerning the chronological succession of Neolithic utensils, pottery and other remains. Here, however, we have been disappointed to a large degree. Paleolithic layers were generally or frequently overlaid by beds of stalagmite or fallen rocks, which have saved them from disturbance. But the Neolithic and Bronze layers are superficial, usually of no great thickness; they have been less solidified and protected, and far more exposed to the disturbing work of burrowing mammals and of men digging for buried treasures. These circumstances, combined with far less continuity of occupation, have greatly diminished the chronological value of their study.

Neolithic cave remains occur in somewhat limited areas scattered all over Europe.[1] They

[1] C: 258.

have been studied in England, France, Spain, Austria, and Germany in at least fairly large numbers. In Austria the cave province extends through Galicia, Moravia, and Bohemia. Here we find primitive pottery; rude stone and numerous bone implements; domesticated cattle, goats, and pigs. Game was evidently very abundant. The cave-dwellers, apparently, were pioneers in the less habitable regions, living mostly by hunting and fishing, from the increase and products of their herds, and from agriculture to a far less degree. The pottery and implements remind us somewhat of those of the earliest lake-dwellings. But we often find bits of copper and bronze, suggesting a later date or a series of inhabitants whose relics have become much mixed. It would not be at all surprising if primitive manufactures had remained here longer in use than in less isolated regions. A deposit of quite similar general character has been found at Duino, near Monfalcone, at the head of the Gulf of Trieste.

A second province lies in Bavaria, between Bamberg and Baireuth. Hoernes considers its remains as also of the same age as the oldest lake-dwellings, but with peculiarities due to the different geographical conditions. The cave provinces of other countries are equally interesting.

Every one has its own features and problems. We would naturally expect that these cave-dwellers would represent the least progressive and prosperous members of the population of any country. In our general survey we can afford to give them only a hasty glance. We can easily understand that where chalk or other soft rock occurred artificial grottos were often excavated.[1]

Remains of dwellings are common all over Europe, and are likely to be uncovered wherever excavations are made in grading or for the foundations of buildings. They are of two forms: the rectangular house and the round hut. The rectangular form is the rule in the lake-dwellings, though with exceptions; on the land the reverse is true. The pit-dwelling at Campigny was elliptical in form with a longest diameter of 4.30 metres. We remember that the settlement at Campigny is probably little, if at all, younger than the shell-heaps. But by far the commoner form of pit-dwelling is circular, with a diameter rarely exceeding two metres. Such small circular pits are exceedingly common. At the bottom we find ashes, bones of animals, implements, and fragments of clay once forming a part of the superstructure, baked hard when

[1] 76.

the hut was burned, and still having marks of
the twigs and branches over which the clay had
been plastered. We picture to ourselves the
hut as mostly underground, with a diameter
usually not exceeding one and one-half to two
metres, excavated to a depth of one or two metres, the pit often surrounded by a rude wall of
field stones. In the centre was the hearth.
The superstructure was merely a cone composed
of a framework of poles interlaced with branches
and twigs plastered with clay. In the primitive
hut there was no perpendicular side wall above
ground, though in some the roof may have been
raised somewhat on the earth thrown out from
the pit. Such differences of detail are of slight
importance. The huts are of all ages. They
were probably erected far back in Paleolithic
time. They seem to be figured in Magdalenian
cave-frescoes.[1] Even the Chellean hunters could
hardly have erected more primitive shelters.
But equally rude huts are still inhabited in the
Balkan Peninsula,[2] and are described by classical
writers as inhabited by the Germans.

Says Tacitus (*Germania*, XLVI) of the Finns
of his day: "They lead a vagrant life: their food
the common herbage; the skins of beasts their
only clothing; and the bare earth their resting-

[1] 40: 283.   [2] B: 53.

place. . . . To protect their infants from the fury of wild beasts and the inclemency of the weather, they make a kind of cradle amidst the branches of trees interwoven together, and they know no other expedient. The youth of the country have the same habitation, and amidst the trees old age is rocked to rest. Savage as this way of life may seem, they prefer it to the drudgery of the field, the labor of building, and the painful vicissitudes of hope and fear, which always attend the defense and the acquisition of property. Secure against the passions of men, and fearing nothing from the anger of the gods, they have attained that uncommon state of felicity, in which there is no craving left to form a single wish. The rest of what I have been able to collect is too much involved in fable. . . ."

Let us hope that the reports which Tacitus had been able to collect concerning the dwellings, as well as the ferocity, filth, and poverty of the Finns, were somewhat exaggerated. Evidently conical, largely subterranean huts have been common in Europe down to far later than Neolithic times. The age of any pit-dwelling can be determined only by its contents.

In addition to these circular pits, long or short trenches occur. Forrer found at Stutzheim one cellar more than ten metres long, and varying from one to three metres in width, with several lateral enlargements as pantries and storehouses.[1] Forrer considers this as the home of the chief man, the "manor-house" of the settlement. Around it he found remains of huts such as we have already described. Frequently space for storage as well as dwelling was gained by clustering small huts. This plan would have had the advantage of protection against loss of everything by fires, which must have been frequent. Such cramped dwellings, with the garbage scattered over the bottom of the hut, or in the huts of the most highly cultured deposited in a special hole in one corner, could hardly have been attractive, clean, or sanitary. But they were cool in summer and warm in winter, and afforded protection against wind and weather. People asked and expected no more. Housekeeping was simple, if not easy. But we can imagine that the return of spring, allowing them to emerge from their burrows, must have been hailed with delight.

We have still much to learn concerning these Neolithic dwellings. They have been discovered by chance, and usually studied only hastily and superficially. A pit discovered and examined may have been only one of a large clus-

[1] E: 139.

ter or village, of which the rest remained undiscovered. Wooden houses of logs, or with a
strong frame of poles seem to have existed in
Bronze, or even late Neolithic times. Sophus
Müller[1] describes settlements in Denmark where
the abundance of ashes and utensils prove long-
continued habitation, and yet no pits seem to
have been found — this may be due to insuf-
ficient investigation — strongly suggesting, at
least, houses entirely above ground builded of
perishable materials. It is very hard to believe
that even a Neolithic family could have lived
through the winter in one, mainly subterranean,
dwelling only two metres in diameter, with a
fireplace in the middle. They would have
been compelled to sleep sitting or standing!
Probably Stutzheim and other similar settlements which have been discovered, represent
the real general average of pit-dwellings, while
besides these there were many of far superior
style and comfort. The development of the
Greek house is still a problem, much more that
of a North German dwelling.

As an example of late Neolithic settlement of
the better or best class, we may take Grosgartach, near Heilbronn, in the Neckar valley.[2]
Here, where now are low meadows, was once a

[1] G: 198; J: 15.   [2] 83.

lake connected with the Neckar. The Neolithic village was carefully and skilfully explored by Hofrath Schliz, whose report is a model of careful observation and clear description.

The situation was very favorable, with loess-clad hills sloping to rich meadows, and the lake furnishing fish and a line of communication. The areas occupied by the houses and stalls were clearly marked by the dark "culture-earth" contrasting sharply with the yellow loess. The principal house was rectangular. The outer wall was composed of posts with a wattling of twigs. This was plastered with clay, mixed with chaff and straw. The inner face of the wall was smoothly finished, and then "kalsomined" reddish yellow, and still further decorated with fresco in geometrical designs. The house — 5.80 metres by 5.35 metres — was divided into two rooms. The larger part of the house was occupied by the kitchen, with its floor about one metre below the surface of the ground, and entered by an inclined plane or ramp. The other chamber, the sleeping-room, was nearly a metre above the kitchen and separated from it by a partition. Benches cut out of the loess were found in both kitchen and sleeping-room. Stalls for cattle and barns or granaries were also found.

Virchow, in his review of Schliz's monograph, emphasizes the fact that apparently Grosgartach was deserted by its inhabitants and fell into decay without leaving any signs of destruction by fire or violence.

The villages of Butmir, Lengyel, Jablanica, and others in southeastern Europe show us a condition of advanced culture here also.[1] Déchelette, speaking of the culture of this region, notices "the striking analogies between these old walled villages of the Balkans and the Danube valley, and those of the Ægean villages of the Troad and Phrygia." Primitive idols, painted pottery, frequent use of the spiral in decorative art, all these reappear here and there in the Neolithic stations of southeastern Europe, and in the eastern basin of the Mediterranean in pre-Mycenæan and Mycenæan days. Evidently houses, settlements, modes of life, and stages of culture differ greatly during the same epoch of the Neolithic period in different parts of Europe. Italy was always far in advance of Europe north of the Alps. But even in northern Europe there was great diversity. Shell-heap dwellers still remained long after a much higher culture prevailed throughout most of Denmark. The life and thought of the pioneer hunters of northern

[1] **B.** See Bibliography.

Germany, and still more of northern Russia, were very different from those of the agriculturists along the valley of the Danube and in the Balkan Peninsula. In Greece little city-states began to arise early. Even in northern Europe density of population and size of settlements varied greatly. One illustration of these differences can be seen in the occurrence of fortified villages and refuges.[1] The age of these fortifications is as great a problem as that of the remains found in a pit-dwelling. The village may be, probably usually is, much older than the surrounding wall, and an earthen wall may contain Neolithic or even perhaps Paleolithic implements. The custom of fortifying villages evidently spread rapidly during the Bronze and Iron periods. Sophus Müller tells us that all walled settlements north of the Alps are far younger than the Neolithic period.[2] This statement, often disputed or neglected, is probably an exaggeration, but may well be true of the region surrounding the Baltic. The sparse and scattered hunting and pioneer population of Scandinavia and Germany had no need of building permanent walls around their single houses or small villages. They had very little wealth to protect.

[1] I: 368.　　　　[2] H: 68.

But an agricultural population inhabiting a fertile region open to attack might well surround their villages with a wall, or provide a burg, or fortified place or "refuge," whither they might drive their cattle or transport their grain. Examples of this are Stutzheim and Urmitz, in the Rhine valley, always a great thoroughfare, and in Switzerland and along the maritime Alps villages of this sort seem to have been fairly frequent. Apparently they were still more numerous in the valley of the Danube and in the Balkan Peninsula. It is not at all surprising to find them in Thessaly, so near to the advanced civilization of Greece.

Another class of settlements usually well protected were the workshops (ateliers) and manufacturing villages, especially those where flint was mined, or where flint implements were made in large quantities and distributed by trade over wide areas.[1] During the Neolithic period these settlements would have held much the same place and importance as our centres of coal, iron, manufacturing, and business have with us to-day. Grand Pressigny and Camp de Chassey, in France, and Cissbury, in England, are single examples of a great number of such fortified mining and manufacturing villages.

[1] A: I, 351.

For a further study of these very interesting remains the reader is referred to the manuals of Déchelette and Hoernes.

Even before the close of the Paleolithic period tundra and steppe were giving place to forests, which were advancing even into Scandinavia. The forest looms large and terrible in the works of classical writers and German antiquarians. Says Tacitus: "Who would leave the softer climes of Asia, Africa, or Italy to fix his abode in Germany, where Nature offers nothing but scenes of ugliness, where the inclemency of the seasons never relents? . . . The face of the country, though in some parts varied, presents a cheerless scene, covered with the gloom of forests, or deformed with wide-extended marshes." He says that the soil produces grain and is well stocked with cattle, though of small size. But grain does not grow in primeval forests, and herds of cattle need at least open glades for pasturage. It is an extreme picture tinged by the homesickness of a citizen of sunny Italy. Northern Europe was generally heavily forested until long after Tacitus's time. The Romans began in earnest the work of deforesting France, and the work was carried on all over Europe in mediæval times. The Neolithic immigrants probably made small clearings with

the aid of fire, especially where the trees were
low and not too thick, as on many light-soiled
areas. They could make but little impression
on the heavy forest growth, though they could
limit its spread. They probably did not need
to make wide clearings of dense forest. There
were many open stretches of country of greater
or less extent awaiting occupants and culture.
This was true especially of districts occupied by
the loess, whose origin from dust drifted by
Paleolithic wind-storms we have already noticed.

Geikie describes loess as typically a "fine-
grained, yellowish, calcareous, sandy loam, consisting very largely of minute grains of quartz
with some admixture of argillaceous and calcareous matter."[1] It is for the most part a
wind-blown deposit. It is widely developed
over low-lying regions, but sweeps up to heights
of 200 to 300 feet and more above the bottoms
of the great river valleys. Again, in many
places we find it heaped up under the lee of
hills, the exposed windward slopes of which bear
no trace of it. Wherever there is loess we are
likely to find the remains of steppe plants and
animals. The ancient steppe area which generally covers, and probably extends considerably

[1] 42: 122; 60; 110: I, 6-13.

beyond, the loess district, is the region occupied by most of the primitive settlements. Even to-day it is less wooded than the rest of northern Europe. Such steppe regions in the North German plain are the great diluvial river terraces, especially the terraces of the Saale and Elbe and the eastern edge of the Harz Mountains; in South Germany the lower Alpine "Vorland" from Switzerland to lower Austria, the uplands of Suabia and Franconia, the valleys of the Main and Neckar, and much of northern Bohemia. These steppe regions of Germany, northern Austria, and Switzerland extended southeastward in a zone following the Danube, widening out in the great Hungarian plain into the vast steppe region extending eastward from the Black Sea or Pontus. From this Pontic steppe a band of more or less open country extended northward along the Carpathians until it almost or quite joined the open regions of the Elbe and along the Harz. A farther extension of this same band seems to have opened the way from the Harz region through northwest Germany into Belgium and northern France, and very probably into Brittany. We see at once the importance of these long lines of open or thinly forested country to the immigrations

and settlement of Neolithic peoples.   Periodical
floods or other conditions kept open many river
valleys, whose importance we shall estimate in
a later chapter.   All this land, except the uplands of Suabia and Franconia, and some similar areas, was comparatively fertile, the loess
areas particularly so, and suited to a primitive
agriculture.

In England the valleys of the Thames and
other rivers were heavily wooded and not populated until much later.   But the long lines of
chalk-downs and oolitic uplands were far less
favorable to forest growth.   In Norfolk and
Suffolk there were apparently open spaces.
Yorkshire and Derbyshire had very similar
landscapes.   The forest was held back wherever
the porous chalk formation made a large out-
crop.   In these places man could settle and find
pasturage for his flocks and attempt a poor sort
of agriculture, even in Neolithic days.   Hence
we find these regions dotted with Neolithic settlements.   The immigrants who came in during the Bronze period settled in the same regions.   Here again clearing of the forest on
any large scale was apparently not attempted
until Roman times, but along its boundaries,
where the forest growth was not too heavy,

these primitive agriculturists may well have cut off the lighter growth for fuel and buildings, and thus have gradually appreciably extended the arable area.

CHAPTER IV

LAKE–DWELLINGS

THE winter of 1853–1854 was exceedingly cold and dry. The surface of the Swiss lakes sank lower than at any time during many preceding centuries. The lowering of the water tempted the inhabitants along the shore to erect dikes and thus fill in the newly gained flats. During this process the workmen along the edge of the retreating water came upon the tops of piles, and between those great quantities of horn and stone implements and fragments of pottery. Aeppli, a teacher in Obermeilen, called the attention of the Antiquarian Society in Zurich to these discoveries. The society recognized at once their importance, and under the leadership of its president, Ferdinand Keller, began a series of most careful investigations which have contributed more to our knowledge of life during the Neolithic period than any discoveries before or since.

The number of these lake-dwellings is very large. Lake Neuchatel has furnished over 50; Lake Leman (Geneva) 40; Lake Constance over

40; Lake Zurich 10. The shores of the smaller lakes have also contributed their full quota.[1] In some of the lakes where the shore was favorable, remains of a lake-dwelling have been found before almost every modern village. Sometimes we find the remains of two villages, one somewhat farther out than the other. In these cases the one nearer the shore is the older, usually Neolithic, while the one farther out belongs to the Bronze period.

These settlements are by no means limited to Switzerland. They stretch in a long zone along the Alps from Savoy and southern Germany through Switzerland into Austria.[2] Herodotus mentions them in the Balkan Peninsula. The amount of bronze seems to increase as we pass from east to west. They are found frequently in the Italian lakes, mostly containing relics of the Bronze Age, though here the western settlements contain little or no metal. A second series has been discovered in Britain and northern Germany, and extending into Russia. These are considerably younger. The scheme of the lake-dwelling was used in historic times in Ravenna and Venice. Large numbers are still inhabited in the far east.

A sunny, sheltered shore, protected by hills

[1] 97: 11, 19.   [2] 95: 102.

from storms and action of waves, was always an attractive site.[1] The character of the land, if open and suitable for pasturage and cultivation, was doubtless important. Much depended on the character of the bottom. Where the shore shelved off gradually and was composed of marl or sand, the piles could be easily driven, and could hold their place firmly. Even if the shore was somewhat too hard and the piles could be driven only a little distance, they were strengthened by piles of stones, often brought from a considerable distance. When a suitable location had been discovered and selected the trees were felled partly by the use of stone axes, and partly by fire, and one end of the log was pointed by the same means, according to Avebury. Their diameter was from three to nine inches, and their length from fifteen to thirty feet. During the Bronze period larger trees were felled and split, and larger piles had to be used in the deeper water farther from the shore.[2]

These rudely sharpened piles were driven into the bottom by the use of heavy stone mallets. This must have involved an immense amount of hard labor, for at the settlement of Wangen 50,000 piles were used, though not all probably

[1] 91: 475. [2] L: 190.

at the same time. Messikommer calculated that at Robenhausen over 100,000 were used. We find sometimes a different foundation. It consists of a solid mass of mud and stones, with erect and also horizontal logs binding the whole structure firmly together. This is evidently a ruder, simpler, and perhaps more primitive, mode of building. It was less suited to an open situation, exposed to heavy waves, and seems to occur more often in smaller lakes now often filled with peat.[1] Wauwyl and Nieberwyl are good illustrations of such a *"Packwerkbau."* Some have considered them as originally floating rafts.

When the piles had been firmly driven, crosspieces were laid over the top, and on this a "flooring" of smaller poles, or of halved logs or even split boards, whose interstices were probably filled with moss and clay, forming a solid and fairly even surface, on which the dwellings could be erected. The framework of the houses was of small piles, some of which have been found projecting considerably above the platforms.[2] "The size of the house is further marked out by boards forced in between the piles and resting edgeways on the platform, thus forming what at the present day we should call

[1] B: 251.   [2] 91: 8.

the skirting boards (mop-boards) of the hut or
rooms. The walls or sides were made of a wat-
tle or hurdle work of small branches, woven in
between the upright piles, and covered with a
considerable thickness of loam or clay." This
is proved by numbers of pieces of clay half-
burnt, or hardened in the fire, with the impres-
sions of the wattle-work still remaining. These
singularly illustrative specimens are found in
nearly every settlement which has been destroyed by fire. The houses were rectangular
except in a few cases. They were apparently
thatched with straw or reeds. The hearths
consisted of three or four stone slabs.

These houses were calculated by Messikommer at Robenhausen to have been about 27 by
22 feet, a very respectable size. One was excavated at Schussenried, whose side-walls and
floor were fairly well preserved. This was a
rectangle about 33 by 23 feet (10 by 7 metres),
and was divided into two chambers. The front
room, 6½ by 4 metres, opened by a door facing
south, and with remains of a hearth in one corner. The rear room, 6½ by 5 metres, was
without outer door, and was apparently a bed-
room.[1] Beside these houses, or forming a part
of them, were stalls for the cattle, granaries,

[1] 96: 366.

and probably work-shops. (The distribution of different remains is well shown in Keller's *Lake Dwellings*, I, p. 45.) The stone and bone implements, and the pottery of the lake-dwellers can be more conveniently considered in connection with those of other regions.

We pass now to the remains of animals and plants found here, especially in their relations to the food supply of the people.[1] Altogether about 70 species of animals have been discovered. Of these 10 are fish, 4 reptiles, 26 birds, and 30 mammals, of which 6 were probably domesticated. The largest of these were the great *Cervus alces* or moose — sometimes called elk — the wild cattle, and the stag (*Cervus elaphus*). Bones of the stag and ox are very numerous and equal those of all others together. Of the horse very few remains are found until the Bronze period. Wild horses seem to have lived on in certain parts of Europe until a late date, but apparently they had emigrated almost altogether from this region. The horse of the Bronze Age was domesticated. The lion had left this region, but lingered on in the Balkans down to historic times. The brown bear and the wolf still roamed in the forest. In the oldest lake-dwellings the bones of wild animals

[1] L: 199; 96: 265; D: 452; 97: 45-60.

make up a far larger proportion of the remains than in the latest ones.

We find a somewhat small dog (*Canis familiaris palustris*) closely resembling that of the Danish shell-heaps. It was apparently of the jackal type, and much like the modern Spitz. This would have been an excellent watch-dog to give warning of the approach of enemies. But at the close of the Neolithic, with the increase of flocks of sheep, a larger dog more closely related to the wolf seems to have spread widely through the country (*Canis familiaris matris optimæ Juit.*). This form was much like, and probably the ancestor of, our present sheep-dogs. A third form (*Canis intermedius*) also occurs. The origin and relationships of the various forms of this oldest domesticated animal are still anything but clear. That they all go back to the jackal and the wolf rather than to a form like the Australian dingo, still seems to be most generally accepted. (But see Schenk.[1])

Man gained the dog by domesticating the jackal and different species of wolves in different parts of the world and then by crossing, or, by a more or less unconscious selection, bred different varieties, until we have at present a chaos of intermingled forms. Something sim-

[1] 97: 47; 96: 289.

ilar but on a smaller scale was true of the domestic cattle. One kind of domestic cattle appears fully domesticated in the oldest lake-dwellings. It is unlike any wild European form. This is the *Bos brachyceros*. It was almost certainly imported. Mingled with its forms we find those of the *Bos primigenius*, a native of Europe and North Asia, but apparently not domesticated. This is the urus, which was common in Europe in Cæsar's day, and lasted in central Europe until 1000 A. D. and still lingers in Poland.[1] This was a very large and powerful form with long spreading horns, whose domestication appears to have commenced toward the close of the Neolithic period. It is not improbable that it was domesticated, or at least tamed, independently in different countries at quite different times. Raising of cattle was at its height during the Bronze Age; afterward the results seem to decline and the cattle to degenerate.

One of the Vaphio vases of about 1500 B. C. represents the capture of large, long-horned cattle in a net, while the second shows similar animals tamed. Apparently the smaller and lighter brachyceros was first tamed, and this success led to a series of experiments with the larger and more difficult form.[2]

[1] 135; C: 65 and 116.   [2] 97.

If we draw a line from northwestern Russia diagonally across Europe southwestward to the mouth of the Rhone, it will divide fairly well the distribution of the descendants of those two forms. To the eastward in Russia and Austria, also generally through Germany, and extending also along the shores of the Baltic, we find the large, heavy, usually long-horned descendants of the *primigenius* stock. The cattle of Spain, and southward into Africa, of France and England, are more of the short-horned, light-built, smaller brachyceros type. Holstein and Jersey are good representatives of the two types, though the Holsteins are, perhaps, a somewhat marked variety. Some regard the cattle of the Scotch highlands as the best representatives of the *primigenius* type, though reduced in size. This same type, on account of its size and endurance of harsh climate, has furnished the range cattle of our Western plains.

Two fairly distinct forms of swine occur in the lake-dwellings. The first is the so-called turbary pig (*Sus scrofa palustris*). This is a small form with comparatively long legs. It differs markedly from the wild boar, and was probably imported already domesticated. Being more or less left to feed and shift for itself, it may well have declined in size from its primitive oriental ancestors. Remains of the larger European wild boar (*Sus scrofa ferus L.*) also occur from the beginning as products of the hunt. But during the Bronze period domesticated descendants of this variety grow numerous, and are crossed with the smaller turbary pig.

"The domestic sheep," says Brehm, "is a quiet, gentle, patient, simple, will-less, cowardly, wearisome animal. It has no character. It understands and learns nothing; is incapable of helping itself." [1] It is certainly absolutely dependent upon man for guidance and protection. This lies partly in its inherited nature and original surroundings, but suggests long domestication. Like the goat, it is originally a mountain form, but adapts itself readily to the dry herbage of the steppe. It is not a native of central Europe but introduced. It is much rarer than the goat in the oldest lake-dwellings, but gradually becomes more abundant, especially in the Bronze period.

The turbary sheep (*Ovis aries palustris*) is very small, with slender legs, long narrow skull, and bones somewhat like those of the goat. It was certainly not developed in Switzerland, and before it arrived there it had apparently been much modified by conditions of life or by cross-

[1] Quoted in **135**: chap. III, 116.

ing. Its anatomical characteristics are made
up of at least three wild forms. The first of
these is the goat-like maned sheep (*Ovis trage-
laphus*) ranging over the mountains of northern
Africa, extending across into Abyssinia. This
form seems to have been domesticated in Egypt
before the middle of the fourth millennium. At
a much later date, in Homeric times, herds of
sheep of a similar form were kept in Greece. It
was much larger than the turbary form.

The arkal (*Ovis arkal*) is the steppe sheep of
central and western Asia. It is the ancestor
of the oriental and African fat-tailed sheep.
The western Asiatic forms seem to have developed the fine wool at the expense of the coarse
hair, like that of the goat and of many other
forms.

A third form is the Moufflon, of the mountains
around the Mediterranean and of its larger
islands — here probably introduced. Similar
forms appear in Europe during the Bronze
period.

Other species are found in different parts of
Asia. The balance of probabilities seems to
incline toward the view that the turbary sheep
came into Europe from western and central
Asia with other "turbary" forms, that it had
been long domesticated, and either here or on

its westward migration may have more or less crossed with the descendants of other varieties. The oldest domesticated goats seem to be descended from the Bezoar goat (*Capra œgagrus*), from the mountains of southwestern Asia.

The presence of oxen, sheep, and goats is enough to prove that the people must have practised agriculture to some extent to have kept these animals alive through the winter. That they were kept on the platform is shown by the presence of manure in the remains underneath. Whether this was used for fertilizer we do not know, nor their method of cultivating the ground. No agricultural implements have come down to us.

"The small-grained, six-rowed barley (*Hordeum hexastichum sanctum*) and the small lake-dwelling wheat (*Triticum vulgare antiquorum*) were the most ancient, most important, and most generally cultivated farinaceous seeds of our country. Next to them come the beardless compact wheat (*T. vulg. compactum muticum*) and the larger six-rowed barley (*Hordeum hexastichum densum*), with the two kinds of millet, the common millet (*Panicum miliaceum*) and the Italian millet (*Setaria italica*). The Egyptian wheat (*Triticum turgidum L.*), the two-rowed wheat (emmer, *Triticum dicoccum Schr.*),

and the one-grained wheat (*Trit. monococcum*)
were probably, like the two-rowed barley, only
cultivated as experiments in a few places; and
the spelt (*Triticum spelta L.*), which at present
is one of the most important cereals, and the
oat (*Avena sativa L.*) appeared later, not till
the Bronze Age, while rye was entirely unknown
among the lake-dwellings of Switzerland."[1]

Oats occur in the Bronze period in western,
middle, and northern Europe, in the Alpine
lake-dwellings, and in the Danish islands. The
ancient Egyptians and Hebrews, Indians and
Chinese, did not cultivate them; they were
raised in Asia Minor and America only since historic times. We remember that wheat and barley are mentioned in the oldest records of the
Old Testament — as in Gideon's barley loaf —
but rye and oats not at all.

The grains seem to show a gradual improvement in productiveness from the very oldest
settlements to those of the Bronze period. They
are found charred and perfectly preserved
wherever the houses were destroyed by fire.
Even the ears and stalks have been saved for
us in the same manner. Charred loaves of
bread, and cake made of poppy-seeds, were also
found. "Bread was made only of wheat and

[1] **91**: 519; **141**.

millet, the latter with the addition of some
grains of wheat, and, for the sake of flavoring
it, with linseed also. Bread made of barley has
not yet been found, and it is probable that barley was chiefly eaten boiled, or more probably
parched or roasted."[1] Flint sickles made of a
long flake set at a right angle with the wooden
handle have been found in Denmark, and others
whose blade is formed by a row of small, sharp
flints set in the edge of a wooden block occur in
Egypt. The hand-mills or mealing-stones are
very abundant, as might be expected.

The occurrence of the seeds of the Cretan
catchfly (*Silene cretica L.*) is interesting, as it
is not found wild in Germany or in southeastern
Europe, but over all the countries of the Mediterranean. Similarly, the corn-bluebottle (*Cen-
taura cyanus L.*) is found wild in Sicily. This
seems to show that these plants came in with
the wheat from Italy. But it is still possible
that both Switzerland and Italy received them
from a source somewhat or considerably farther
east or south.

Apples and pears, split and dried, occur abun-
dantly. Some of the apples are so large that
they suggest a certain amount of care and cultivation. Sour crabapples, and the stones of

[1] 91: 521.

cherries, plums, and sloes are found accompanied
by the seeds of the wild grape; of elderberries,
raspberries, blackberries, and strawberries.
Acorns, beechnuts, and hazelnuts were stored up.
Besides the seeds of the poppy, already mentioned, those of caraway were used apparently
to flavor the bread. Altogether some 170 plants
have been discovered and determined from these
localities.[1]

Basket-making and the weaving of mats from
bast-fibres had led up to a highly developed
weaver's art. Few or no remains of wool have
come down to us from Neolithic time, though
it occurs in graves of the Bronze Age farther
north. It would not preserve by charring, as
all other lake-dwelling organic remains have
been saved for us, and our failure to discover
it is not surprising. We can hardly believe
that these people did not use the wool of their
flocks of sheep, or failed to felt the hair of their
goats. But flax has been found in all stages
of preparation and manufacture in great quantities. Says Messikommer of Robenhausen:
"Every house had its loom." We find not only
threads, cords, and ropes, twine and nets, but
cloth of varying pattern and design. Some
pieces were so finely woven and well preserved

[1] 96: 295.

that their discoverers could hardly believe that they were not of modern make. Fringes and embroidery occur.[1]

Linen alone could hardly have furnished sufficient protection against the cold and dampness of the Swiss winter climate. The more primitive inhabitants had an abundance of furs. Garments of sheepskin were doubtless in use. And probably wool and goat's-hair were woven or felted into outer garments. Dye-stuffs of black, yellow, red, and blue coloring furnished a variety of tints and shades.

Very few human bones have been found among those lake-dwelling remains; and only a few burial-places, or rather tombs, in the neighboring mainland. The discussion of their mode of burial and racial characteristics may well be deferred to a later chapter.

Of their religious cult we know almost nothing.[2] No idols or fetiches have been recognized. Certain "crescents" of clay, supported with the horns turned upward, have been considered by some as head-rests, for which purpose they are still used by certain African tribes. Others have considered them as representatives of the crescent moon; still others as conventionalized ox heads and horns. It seems highly probable

[1] 95: 175.　　　　[2] L: 222; 91: 175–178, 338.

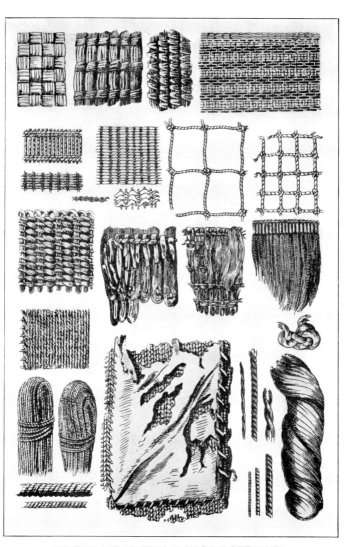

WEAVING AND PLAITING FROM LAKE-DWELLINGS

that they had some religious significance, but its exact nature is still uncertain. We shall return to them later.

A lake-dwelling of any size is inconceivable without a well-advanced social development. It could hardly be founded, builded, or maintained without close co-operation. Families had to live closely crowded together, almost as in our modern cities. Neighbors had learned to get on with one another and live together in peace, and to submit to a close regulation or discipline by law or custom. They seem to have been a peaceful folk and exposed to no great dangers from outside attack, at least in Neolithic time. When the ice fringed the shores or covered the small lakes, they must have been easily open to attack. A few brands thrown into the thatched roof would have brought sure destruction. Traces of conflagration occur, as at Robenhausen, which was twice destroyed by fire.[1] But these occurrences are rare. Neolithic settlements seem to have been more frequently abandoned because of the growth of peat than by any sudden or violent destruction. Conditions probably changed in this respect during the Bronze period.

Their food was varied and more than fairly

[1] 91: 47.

abundant. They had their domestic animals to furnish flesh, milk, probably butter and cheese. Agriculture was primitive, but in some cases we find large stores, we might say granaries, of wheat; and wild fruits and vegetable foods were abundant. The forests offered game, and the lakes were well-stocked with fish. There may have been times of hardship and dearth, but famine could hardly have ravaged a people with these three sources of supply.

The lake offered a thoroughfare for their canoes, and communication was easy for long distances. To cite only one illustration: flint was brought from Grand Pressigny, in France, and manufactured in certain Swiss localities. There was much variety and division of labor between different villages. One manufactured flint very largely — so at and around Moosseedorf; while Robenhausen and Wangen have furnished great quantities of cloth. Others were rather centres for the manufacture of pottery. Even in the same village one area is richer in one product, a second in another. There was much variety as well as freedom of intercommunication. The whole region lay a little back from the great Danube thoroughfare, but near enough to it to retain connection with the larger world. Life was not altogether monotonous.

The lake-dwellings have been divided according to their age into three groups or stages, representing three epochs more or less marked.[1]

Stage I. Archaic Epoch.—Axes small and made out of indigenous material. "Hammer-axes" and utensils of horn and bone rude. No decorations on weapons, utensils, nor on the crude pottery. Plaiting and weaving practised. Population in Switzerland at this time seems to have been sparse. Food obtained from hunt more than from domestic animals. Examples: Chavannes (Schafis) Moosseedorf, Wauwyl. People brachycephalic.

Stage II. Middle Neolithic Epoch.—Weapons and utensils more perfect. Stone axes finely polished, often with hole for handle, sometimes very large. Beside the commoner minerals five to eight per cent of implements made of nephritoids (nephrite, jadeite, and chloromelanite). These are almost absent in Epochs I and III. Pottery of far better material and manufacture, with traces of ornament. Remains of domestic and wild animals nearly equal. Domestic animals are turbary pig, goat, sheep, turbary cattle, but *primigenius* form present though less common. Brachycephalic and dolichocephalic people nearly equal in number. Examples: Robenhausen and Concise.

[1] **95**: 135; **96**: 189, 219, 191.

Stage III. Copper Epoch.—Hammer-axes, beautifully finished. Bone and horn implements. Nephritoid minerals less used. Pottery more artistic. Cord-decoration appears. Certain ornaments, weapons, and implements are made of copper. Domesticated animals improve and form a larger part of the food than game. Cattle especially increase in numbers, and a new race of sheep has arisen. Long-heads more numerous than broad-heads. Examples: Roseax, at Morges. Locraz, Ferril (Vinelz).[1]

It is interesting to notice that remains of domestic cattle are abundant in all ages, that goats are more abundant than sheep in the earliest lake-dwelling, but that the sheep became equally numerous in the second epoch, while they decidedly outnumbered the goats during the Bronze period. This is what we should expect from the advance of culture.

Says Keller:[2] "The shores of the western portion of Lake Constance are probably more thickly studded with settlements than those of any other Swiss lake. In fact, here are found happily united all the requirements necessary for the erection of dwellings of this nature. A

[1] For a study of examples grouped according to epoch, see **96**: p. 220–264.
[2] **91**: II, 432.

deposit of marl stretches along nearly the whole of its shores and of tolerable breadth. A rich tract of country between the shore and the hills which rise quietly behind; forests of pine and oak; pleasant bays with a gravelly bottom; a great abundance of fish in the lake, and a superfluity of game in the surrounding forests, were circumstances highly favorable to the colonization of these shores."

Could we have sat on one of these village platforms of a summer afternoon and looked out to the wheat-fields on the shore, and seen the canoes come in with fish or game, and the cattle returning from the mainland pasture; could we have watched the men fashioning implements and all manner of woodwork, and the women grinding the grain or moulding pottery, or spinning and weaving; we should have found a great deal to please and interest us. The fruits and berries, the smell of roasting fish and baking bread, of cakes well flavored with the oil from beechnut or flax, or perhaps sifted over with the seeds of poppy or caraway, would have been far from disagreeable. We should have felt that it was a goodly land, and that life was well worth living. We should not have been disturbed by shrieking steamboats, puffing and groaning locomotives, or honking automobiles, or by telegraphs or telephones, by letters which must be answered or books which must be read. There were no stocks and bonds, bills or notes, strikes or lockouts. There was no labor question; all simply had to work. No one went to school, except to nature, and there were no lectures. "The name of that chamber was peace."

We ought not to forget in our comfort that everybody could not live in a lake-dwelling, that all over Europe there were other settlements or dwellings, more lonely or isolated, where food was never abundant and sometimes very scarce, where labor was unremitting and the reward scanty. But even in those less civilized regions there was probably usually much rude comfort; and if there were times of scarcity and want, there were also times of feasting and abundance. All over Europe there were, even in Neolithic time, children, boys and girls playing around the houses; and young men and women looking out on life with the same inexperience and illusions, courage and hopes, which lure us onward to-day.

CHAPTER V

A GLANCE EASTWARD

THE culture of the oldest lake-dwellings appears suddenly in Europe, and its beginnings are exotic in all their essentials. The turbary cattle were quite different from the wild *primigenius* race of the surrounding regions; and we find no remains of the intermediate forms which should occur if domestication had taken place here. The same is true of the turbary pig. Wild sheep are unknown in northern Europe, and the moufflon of the Mediterranean islands can hardly have been the ancestor of our Swiss flocks, and is very possibly descended from domesticated ancestors which reverted to wild life. Something very similar may be said of our oldest cereals, wheat and barley.

We must evidently turn eastward or southward to find the cradle of the whole culture. Even if it came partly from Italy, it could hardly have developed there. Egypt may have made contributions, but mostly at a later date. We naturally turn first to Asia, the great centre of mammalian evolution, probably the oldest seat of cattle-raising and agriculture, cradle of man and centre of his earliest development. The true Neolithic cultures in northern Europe can hardly be older than about 6000 B. C.; the lake-dwellings are probably far younger. We must first inquire into the location, age, and character of the oldest agriculture in nearer Asia, where great discoveries have been made during the last twenty years.

We naturally turn first to Babylonia. Under the temple of Bel, at Nippur, was an immense platform constructed of sun-dried bricks, most of them stamped with the name of Sargon or of Naram Sin. The date of Sargon seems still uncertain; many historians place it at 2800 B. C.; others, and apparently most archæologists, like Obermaier, still hold to the old date, 3750 B. C.[1] Without any attempt to decide this question, we will hold in this chapter to the older date; and believers in the latter date can subtract 1,000 from our figures for earlier times, though this does not apply to Pumpelly's estimates.

Says Delitzsch[2] of this mound: "In the deepest layers of these remains, or what amounts to the same, back many centuries beyond the fifth millennium, everywhere interesting and valuable remains of human civilization come to

[1] D: 527, 549.   [2] 115: 535.

light, fragments of vessels of copper, bronze, and clay, a quantity of earthenware so beautifully lacquered in red and black that we might consider them of Greek origin, or at least influenced by Greek art, had they not been found eight metres deep under Naram Sin's pavement." Here we find the Bronze period, or possibly late Copper, before 5000 B. C. A city with a high and complex culture had already arisen. No one believes that the culture could have originated in the rank, almost untamable, primitive jungle of Mesopotamia. Its beginnings must be sought elsewhere and earlier. But the age and character of Babylonian civilization encourage one to seek further in western Asia.

In 1904 Pumpelly[1] made most thorough and careful investigations at Anau, near Askabad in Turkestan, about 300 miles east of the southeast corner of the Caspian Sea, and 200 miles west of Merv. The remarkable results of his work are described in two large volumes, and have not received the attention which they deserve. He excavated in two large Kurgans or mounds. The north Kurgan is the older and chiefly concerns us. The Neolithic remains occur in thin compact strata aggregating some forty-five feet in thickness. The earliest settle-

[1] 110.

ment was a town covering at least five acres, possibly nearly ten.

At the time of the beginning of the settlement, which Pumpelly estimated as somewhat before 8000 B. C., the inhabitants lived in rectangular houses built of uniform sun-dried bricks. They were skilful potters, though unacquainted with the potter's wheel, making different grades of coarse and fine vessels. These were unglazed, but often painted with a definite series of geometrical patterns. They had the art of spinning, for whorls are found in all strata from the lowest up. They cultivated cereals, for the casts of the chaff of wheat and barley are found in the clay of the thicker pots. At first they had no domestic animals, only the bones of wild forms being found. When ten feet of culture strata had been accumulated the remains of a tame *Bos namadicus*, the Asiatic variety of the *Bos primigenius*, or urus, occurred. That this animal had already been domesticated is inferred from the less compact microscopic structure of the bones modified by artificial conditions. At this time the change of structure, if not complete, was evident. It had been for some time under the new conditions. The turbary pig appears about 7500 B. C.,[1] the turbary

[1] **110**: Plate 5, opposite pp. 50, 67.

sheep about 1500 years later, but preceded by varieties of the great horned mountain sheep. The turbary cattle appear to have been a small variety of the *Bos namadicus*, somewhat dwarfed by drought and hardship.

The camel appears at Anau somewhat after 6000 B. C., and seems to be a means of intercourse and transport far antedating the horse, in a region already showing signs of dessication.

Spherical mace-heads occur reminding us of those used in Egypt. But no lance-head or arrow-point or other stone weapon was found in the lower levels. We do not know how they killed or captured the larger animals; they may have used the sling or bolero. In the lowest strata we find the bones of young children, but not of adults, buried in a contracted position under the floors of the dwellings. The first objects of copper and lead appear about 6000 B. C., and open the Æneolithic period. Pumpelly distinguishes a Copper period, here longer and more distinctly marked than in Europe. The turquoise bead found in one of the graves came, in all probability, from the Iranian plateau, as did probably the copper and lead also.

He has shown us that even on the steppe the cultivation of cereals precedes the domestication of sheep and cattle. The nomadic life follows instead of preceding agriculture. The pioneers in this region cultivated the zone of steppe, into which rivers poured from the mountains. When cattle and sheep and goats had multiplied, the herdsmen drove them farther and farther on the rich pasturage of the boundless steppe. Thus nomads gradually appear. There are also different varieties of nomadism. Nomadic tribes were far less active and dangerous neighbors even after the domestication of the camel than when, about 2000 B. C., they had domesticated the horse. The first herdsman may have differed from the latter nomad almost as much as the most pacific sheep-herder of our Western plains differs from the liveliest cowboy.

Pumpelly's time-estimates have been criticised by Doctor H. Schmidt, of Berlin.[1] He makes the rate of growth far more rapid than Pumpelly thought and shortens the periods. In determining length of periods he relies far more on artifacts and less on probable rate of accumulation. The criticisms seem hardly well founded. Pumpelly's estimate of rate of increase was based upon a careful and broad comparison of accumulations in the deserted city, Anau, in Merv, and other localities. They seem conservative, but we must recognize that such esti-

[1] 111.   Cf. 110: I, 48.

mates are always only approximate. His estimates result in a series of dates generally in
close agreement with those of most students of
oriental archæology.

In the Third Culture Epoch there was found
"copper, with sporadic appearance of low percentage of tin." This describes well the close
of the Copper period or the beginning of the
Bronze Age, the rest of which is not represented
at Anau, the settlement being deserted, probably
because of aridity. Pumpelly thinks that the
last strata deposited before the desertion comes
down to the Bronze Age, and, assuming the
latest possible date for the beginning of this
period, places it about 2200 B. C. This is
almost surely much too late. Obermaier dates
the beginning of the Bronze period at 4000 B. C.[1]
(If we substitute the later date, 2750 B. C., for
Sargon's region, the Bronze period would begin
about 3000 B. C., the date accepted by Montelius.[2]) Pumpelly places the beginning of the
Copper Epoch at 5000 B. C., again agreeing
with Montelius. His estimates seem generally
somewhat too conservative, as he doubtless intended they should be; the earliest remains may
be considerably older than he thought. Investigations made during the last twenty years seem

[1] D: I, 545.   [2] B: II, 242; D: 527.

generally to lead us to believe that the beginnings of Neolithic culture are far older in western Asia than we had supposed, while in middle and northern Europe they are probably somewhat younger than we had thought. In this connection we may well remember that Evans found eight metres of Neolithic remains under the palace at Cnossus, in Crete, and estimated their age at about 14,000 years.

The culture at Anau is very similar in all its essentials to that of the European lake-dwellers, and is much older. The same cereals and the same kinds of domesticated animals appear in both. The brick houses are better and the very fine painted pottery is new and peculiar. These and the art of spinning and the cultivation of cereals were brought hither by the first settlers; their development to this stage must have taken place elsewhere and occupied a long period of time. Sheep could not have been domesticated here, for they and the goats are natives of the mountains, and could not survive wild on the steppe. Neither is the pig a steppe animal, but lives naturally in forest glades and along watercourses. Pumpelly has evidently discovered a very old and interesting station in the spread of this ancient culture, but not its cradle. This was apparently in some mountainous region.

The nearest and most likely place to search for it is somewhere on the Iranian plateau, to which the turquoise bead and the later-introduced copper and lead found at Anau also point.

Here at Susa (Shushan), about one hundred miles from the apex of the Persian Gulf, de Morgan excavated in a mound rising about thirty-four metres above the level of the plain and continuing some six metres below the surface, which has been raised that amount since the first settlement was made.[1] The total thickness of the remains is therefore about forty metres. The lowest strata as yet have been only slightly studied. The uppermost ten to fifteen metres cover a period of about 6,000 years. If the lower strata were accumulated at the same rate, the first settlement was begun about 18,000 years ago at a conservative estimate. Montelius, the best authority on European prehistoric chronology, basing his conclusions on de Morgan's discoveries, places the date of the beginning of Neolithic culture in this part of Asia at about 18,000 B. C., or somewhat earlier.[2]

Over twenty metres of these remains are purely Neolithic. There was the usual abundance of flint nuclei, flakes, and utensils. There

[1] 116–120.   [2] B: II, 168.

was obsidian, evidently brought from a distance — de Morgan thinks from Armenia, a thousand miles away. This is not impossible; we shall find that trade or barter was far more extensive at this time than has usually been supposed.

Here again we find abundant pottery in the lowest strata. It is of a "dark brown pattern painted on a pale ground, partly imitating basketry and textiles, partly rendering plants and animals with childish simplicity. . . . It resembles in a striking way a few widely scattered series which are all that have been secured hitherto from a very ill-explored area: from a Neolithic site underlying the Hittite castle at Sakye-Giezi, in North Syria, from the surface of early mounds in Cappadocia, and from low levels of the Hittite capital, at Boghaz-Keui; and, more surprising still, from an important site, also Neolithic, at Anau, on the northern edge of the Persian plateau looking over into Turkestan; and at a number of points scattered over the flat lowland on the north side of the Black Sea, and thence into the Balkan Peninsula as far south as Macedonia and Thessaly. These resemblances are general and their value may be overestimated; there are differences in detail, but the general similarity seems to link the peoples over this wide area at the same time in one region of kindred art and culture, if not of blood."[1]

The discoveries at Susa and elsewhere in this region seem to prove that compact settlements of fair size had arisen in western Asia long before the founding of Anau.[2] Such settlements could have been formed only by sedentary peoples practising agriculture, not by mere wandering hunters. Our definite knowledge of the domestic animals of Susa is very small. But, as we have just seen, the peculiar, fine, decorated pottery found in the oldest strata of Susa, Anau, and many other localities scattered over a wide area, is certainly a strong argument for believing that an agriculture in general very similar to that of the oldest strata at Anau was wide-spread over the Iranian plateau, Asia Minor, and elsewhere. Where or when it began we do not know. We can only conjecture as to the place and mode of its beginning. It may not be out of place to mention a very general hypothesis of this sort, and this we will now attempt to frame.

The Bühl moraines, in Lake Lucerne, are estimated as having been deposited between 16,000 and 24,000 B. C., during the Early Magdalenian stage of post-glacial time, which would, there-

[1] 124: 121; 123; D: 526.   [2] 116: 195 ff., 197 Bib.

fore, be contemporaneous with the earliest set-tlement at Susa.[1] The climate of Europe was then somewhat colder and much moister than at present. The ice-cap extended much farther south in middle Europe than in Russia or Si-beria. Under these circumstances central Asia probably enjoyed a much moister climate than at present, without extreme cold. The Caspian and Aral Seas occupied a much larger area than at present, and were very likely connected. The Tarim basin may well have been a great lake surrounded by a zone of garden instead of the sandy waste which it is to-day. Conditions of increased moisture would have made the now parched regions of the Iranian plateau an ex-ceedingly rich and favored region. Toward the close of the Post-glacial Epoch the mountains were probably well forested, but alternating dryer times would have brought open glades, with lakes interspersed.

When Europe changed from tundra to forest man became largely a fisherman, more or less settled at some favorable spot, and collecting his vegetable food in all directions. The same may well have been true of life at this early date in Persia. The man hunted or fished, the woman and the children gathered all kinds of

[1] 40: 281.

animals and plant food, berries and other fruits,
acorns and other nuts. One of the richest
sources of food must have been the roots, tubers,
and other underground stems. If there were
any patches of richly seeded grasses or grains
on the near-by glade or hill, we may be sure that
the woman did not fail to beat off the ripe seed
with a stick, and carry it home with her. The
primitive family was not dainty or particular
in its appetite. The women were the first botanists, the first to notice the nutritive, medicinal,
or poisonous qualities of plants, and the first
physicians.[1]

When she turned homeward with her load of
spoil, some berries, seeds, and small bulbs
doubtless fell to the ground and escaped her
notice. These grew and flourished in the richer
soil around the hut or shelter, for all the garbage
could not have accumulated in the hut. Some
unusually observing woman noticed this, and
protected the plants, or even cultivated them a
little with her digging-stick, and pulled out some
of the largest smothering weeds. She began to
plant a few others, and gradually started a garden. The garden is older than the farm, and
hoe and digging-stick vastly older than the
plough. This woman had discovered, and al-

[1] 139: chap. II, 146.

most created, a new world of science and culture which was to revolutionize life.

Rice growing wild in large fields under suitable conditions is still gathered by all savages. This grain needed no preparation except boiling, while wheat and barley must be crushed or ground between stones, probably used at first for grinding dry nuts. Peas and beans, many vetches, and other members of this family so characteristic of the dryer uplands, were gathered very early, and may have been cultivated before wheat. Melons and many of the gourds always must have been eaten. We shall notice later that the zone of Persia and Asia Minor lay on the boundary line between two great botanical provinces, a northern and a southern, and furnished a very wide range of plants for this earliest experiment station.[1] A great variety of plants were tested sooner or later, and only a few of the very best and most capable of improvement have been retained to our day. On the steppe at a later date wheat and barley were most profitable, and most widely cultivated. But even here hoe-culture was for a long time the only mode. It still exists in Africa, Asia, and Japan; and was the only mode of culture known in America at the time of its discovery. Hoe-culture was at first, and has generally re-

[1] M: 217.

mained, woman's work; ploughing with cattle
was a man's job. This had far-reaching results
to which we must return in a later chapter.

But we must not think that the Iranian
plateau, with its great zone of piedmont steppe
stretching eastward and westward along its
northern border across the continent of Asia,
was the only place where agriculture could start
and reach a high degree of development in ancient times. Its possibility lay in the habit
of the woman of collecting the vegetable food
and smaller animals, while the men hunted
and fished. Useful food plants furnishing large
amounts of food are to be found in all continents,
and differ markedly in different soils and climatic zones. Hence even the beginnings of
agriculture were probably not confined to any
one region, but were wide-spread, manifold, and
independent. The Chinese migrating eastward
and southeastward down the great river valleys
from eastern Turkestan may have carried with
them the cultivation of wheat, or adopted it independently. The rice culture of China may
have been borrowed from India or independently evolved. India and the Malay Archi-
pelago and Africa have every one its own agriculture, of whose origin and early development
we know nothing.

But western Asia, or more precisely the Iranian plateau, had another piedmont region beside the zone stretching along its northern border. This second piedmont zone of grass-land, or oasis, as Breasted has pointed out, bends in the form of a horseshoe along the western slope of the Iranian plateau, then northward and westward around the headwaters of the Tigris and the Euphrates, and southward through Syria.[1] Here it dries out in the great Syrian and Arabian deserts. But these also, as well as the Arabian plateau stretching along the Red Sea, may have been well watered and inhabitable in early post-glacial time. The Arabian plateau and its piedmont zone in those days may well have been an independent centre of agricultural development, which gave place to the nomadism so characteristic of the Semitic peoples only at a later date. Of the early history of Arabia we are still completely ignorant. But in the twilight of history we see those Semites coming into the Mesopotamian valley from the west while the Sumerians entered from the east. Those two streams of migration, mingling, founded the great Babylonian Empire, to which all oriental peoples looked up with an awe and reverence, as well as fear, which we can scarcely

[1] 125: 100, *map.*

appreciate. Evidently, and this is the fact of chief importance to us, parts of the nearer east were highly civilized before anything better than savagery had developed in northern Europe.

But far older than these cities of the Mesopotamian river valleys is the culture of the forests, glades, lakes, and riversides of the plateaus. Evidence seems steadily to accumulate that here we are to seek for the beginnings of agriculture and the domestication of animals which were slowly to change the face of the earth and the life and character of man.

Hoe-tillage of the ground is evidently far older than cattle-raising or nomadic life. It had been brought to Anau before 8000 B. C., and had probably already been practised at Susa and elsewhere thousands of years earlier. But we cannot help asking whether other plants may not have been cultivated long before cereals. Roots and tubers are much more conspicuous than the smaller grains. These underground storehouses of nutriment adapted to give the plant a quick and sure start, during a short spring period of growth and flowering, are abundant everywhere. They still form the staple crop in many parts of the world. We remember the potatoes, sweet potatoes, yams, the cassava, and a host of others. In our northern regions we still cultivate beets, turnips, and carrots, though now becoming more and more food for cattle. These plants also are less closely limited to the steppes and plateaus. They occur all through the mountain or shore regions, and for this reason would have been likely to attract the attention of "collectors."

Primitive woman had no plough, only the digging-stick, the agricultural implement of the Australians. Later they learned to make a hoe, sometimes out of a tine of deer's horn, sometimes of stone or other material, something half-way between a hoe and a pick. With such an implement a fair amount of soil could be broken up and well stirred. When domestic animals were introduced into Africa the plough followed only in the eastern regions; all through the rest of Africa the old hoe-culture held its own. Europeans introduced the plough into America. As a means of breaking up the ground the plough is infinitely superior; for tillage and cultivation the hoe is far more useful. When wheat has once been sown it cares for itself; further cultivation is unnecessary — it is the lazy man's crop. Perhaps that, with a touch of the spur of necessity, persuaded the male to undertake ploughing. When the plough was invented many vegetables formerly cultivated probably became less profitable or attractive, and were given up. A revolution took place in agriculture. Probably the plough was at first dragged by women. It is impossible to say just when it was invented. It was used during the Bronze period, for it is represented in rock-carvings of that age. Some stone ploughshares may be Neolithic.

Studying European Neolithic agriculture in the light of the methods of savage and barbarous peoples, or even of our pioneer ancestors, we imagine them living on the border of the forests which furnished food and wood for buildings and implements. The first step was to burn and clear a place where the undergrowth was not too heavy, and to break up the soil with pick or hoe. Here the patch of grain was sowed. The soil fertilized by the ashes gave him a fair crop, but became exhausted after a few years of cultivation, and he was compelled to break up a new field. Some investigators have thought that the lake-dwellers used the manure from their cattle on their fields, but in most parts of Europe cultivation of the soil was probably crude and superficial. On the chalk downs of England, chief places of settlement by Neolithic peoples in this region, we find terraces and narrow strips which may have been prepared at this time, though their age is very uncertain. They often are of a size and form not well adapted to plough-culture. They have a look of permanent occupation. These may well have been fertilized. The evidence is very uncertain. When the loess soil was of fair depth cultivation may have gone on for many years without fertilizers of any sort.

The primitive plough was hardly more than a pointed stout branch or stub of a tree, whose longer fork was fastened to the yoke. It made a furrow triangular in cross-section, broad at the top and narrowing to an edge at the bottom. It did not "turn" a strip, and between two furrows a long ridge was left unbroken. Even in Roman times cross-ploughing was common or usual. Even this rude culture needed the strength of cattle to draw the plough. The plough is associated in our minds with oxen, and the first man who made his cow, instead of his wife, draw the plough was a great benefactor.

Even the domestication of cattle was less easy than it seems at first sight. Wild animals rarely reproduce in captivity. Pumpelly thinks that the way toward the domestication of our larger cattle may have been paved by a long period of drought driving them from the steppe into the better-watered oases, and thus into association

with man. But this could hardly have been
true of the mountain sheep and goats, on which
man may well have experimented before he attempted the more difficult task of domesticating
the larger, more powerful, and less manageable
Bos namadicus. How did man hit upon the plan
of castrating the bull and thus changing this in-
tractable, ugly beast into the docile and patient
ox? There seems to be a good amount of plausi-
bility in Hehn's brilliant suggestion that this
may have come about in connection with some
ancient systems of religious rites and beliefs.[1]
There is nothing impossible or very improbable
in this view. But the very brilliancy of the conjecture and the clearness with which it is expressed, and the wealth of learning used to support it, warns us against too ready acceptance.
We can only confess our complete ignorance and
wait for future discoveries as patiently as we
can.

At present nearly all our knowledge of what
was going on in this dim and remote past must
be gained by a study of savages still holding the
customs of the past in a somewhat or greatly
modified form and spirit. Certain very general
inferences may be made without great danger.
But to frame clear and exact conceptions of life

[1] O: 291.

in these remote ages from these sources would demand a union of the boldest genius with the most wary caution. All these peoples have changed greatly during past millennia both for better and worse, usually probably in the latter direction. Customs have all been modified by changed conditions, surroundings, and inferences. It is exceedingly difficult to distinguish between what is really primitive and what is degenerate, perhaps of comparatively recent origin. The problem bristles with tantalizing questions, which tempt us to spin fascinating hypotheses all the more dangerous because of their attractiveness and apparent simplicity. Our great need is new facts and discoveries, and a clearer knowledge and understanding of old ones.

We may well connect and condense the chief results of our study in this chapter. It seems to be clear that a culture essentially similar to that of the European lake dwellers existed at Anau, in the piedmont zone, a little north or northeast of the Iranian plateau, with which it had trade relations. The oldest turbary forms of domesticated animals appear here at least 1,500 years before the founding of the Swiss lake dwellings. They were mostly introduced from some mountain region, the nearest probable source being the Iranian plateau, but their first domestication may have taken place equally well elsewhere in western or central Asia, or even in Arabia. Susa shows similar remains extending back into a far more remote past; and the similarity or kinship of the pottery in the oldest strata at Susa and Anau and elsewhere leads us to believe that a culture similar in other respects also was widely distributed at this time. We can hardly doubt that agriculture was practised by the founders of all these settlements.

We can only frame conjectures as to the origin of agriculture. It seems to have been introduced by the women of hunting and fishing tribes. The first agricultural implement was probably the digging-stick, which was followed by the hoe. Hoe-culture is still common in Asia and Africa. Finally, during the first part of the Bronze period, or perhaps somewhat earlier, the plough drawn by cattle and guided by a man superseded the hoe as a means of breaking up the soil for the culture of grain.

CHAPTER VI

MEGALITHS

MEGALITHS, those great stone monuments of prehistoric time, have always excited the wonder and interest of all observers.[1] Under the name of dolmens or stone chambers, cromlechs or stone circles, tumuli or mounds, they form a striking contrast to the insignificant and ephemeral thatched huts of wood and clay which formed the homes of the living. These chambers, especially those of later date, are often accompanied by circles or radiating lines of rude pillars, the Menhirs or standing stones. In the more fertile and densely populated regions the great blocks have been removed and used in the foundations of buildings. They must once have been far more numerous. But Déchelette reports nearly 4,500 as still existing in France;[2] England contains almost or quite as many; and they are very numerous in Denmark and Sweden. We will mainly follow Sophus Müller in his study of these monuments in Denmark.[3]

The simplest, and apparently the oldest,

[1] L: chap. V.   [2] A: I, 386.   [3] G: cf. J: 43.

dolmens are the small rectangular chambers consisting of four stones set up on edge with one large one forming the roof. These are usually between 5 and 7 feet in length, 2 to 3½ feet wide, and 3 to 5 feet in height. One of the end stones is shorter, leaving an opening under the roof through which one may reach or even crawl into the chamber. Somewhat larger chambers of the same type and having five or six wall stones are not uncommon.

Even these small chambers were intended for long use, and to contain more than one body; some contain the remains of a dozen. The bones lie in layers covered with flint chips, or in little heaps where they have been collected to give room for new interments. Many of the smaller chambers were too short to allow the body to lie fully extended; in some it was evidently placed in a sitting posture leaning against the wall.

These smaller dolmens were surrounded by a heap of earth reaching nearly to the top of the side stones, but not covering the roof, and hardly deserving to be called a tumulus. The roof was usually composed of one great stone, flat below but arching above and forming a sort of monument. In one chamber this roofstone is eleven feet long and three feet thick.

On each side of the doorway a stone is often set upright to keep back the earth of the tumulus, and a covering stone may be laid across them. Here we have a form intermediate between the small dolmen without entrance-stones and the large chambers, which we shall consider later.

The earthern tumulus may be round in outline or elliptical, forming the long grave — the *Hunnenbett* of popular German speech. The round tumuli rarely exceed 40 feet in diameter. They were as a rule surrounded by a circle of upright stones, now generally removed. The long tumuli are rarely more than 5 or 6 feet high, and 20 to 30 feet wide. The length varies greatly: usually between 50 and 100 feet, but infrequently from 100 to 200 feet; one is 500 feet long with over 100 of the marginal stones still standing.

The chambers in the round and long tumuli in Denmark are very similar, but in the long tumuli there are usually two or more dolmens, often symmetrically located. In other cases it looks as if a tumulus had been lengthened to cover chambers added later. A large amount of variety in such details is not surprising. More rarely we find two or more small tumuli side by side, each with one or two chambers. That those smaller dolmens or chambers are the old-

"CROUCHING BURIAL" (HOCKER–
BESTATTUNG) ADLERBORG,
NEAR WORMS

MENHIR, CARNAC, BRITTANY

DOLMEN, HAGA, ISLAND OF BORUST

est is suggested not only by their simplicity but even more by the pottery and implements contained in them, though this is not invariably true, as the small dolmens continued in use throughout the Neolithic period, in some regions far later. The gifts which they contain are usually not numerous and often very scanty.

The wide distribution of these simplest stone monuments is exceedingly interesting. They occur in Denmark and Sweden, in North Germany and Holland, in Great Britain and France, Portugal and Spain, in North Africa, in the Ægean Islands, in Palestine and farther eastward, in Thrace and Crimea, along the eastern shore of the Black Sea. They are very numerous in India.[1] Throughout this wide extent they agree not only in general form and structure, but also in certain interesting details. For instance, the oriental and southern dolmens frequently have a round opening in the upper part of the slab closing the entrance, corresponding to the wide opening above the door of the Scandinavian dolmens. The difference in the form of the opening may be explained by the difficulty of cutting a circular opening in the hard granite rocks of the northern area. There was a general unity of thought in essentials, espe-

[1] A: 421.

cially in those oldest forms. There was much diversity in execution or expression in later structures. Some of them took the form of pyramids in Egypt. In Mycenæ we find the "Tomb of Atreus," a magnificent building in the form of a beehive. The large chambers, "Giant Chambers" or *Riesenstuben* of northern Europe, especially of France, are connected with the older small dolmens by many intermediate forms. For example, if another pair of stones is added to the sides of a fair-sized dolmen, we have a chamber six to eight feet in length. Such dolmens always have a covered entrance to the doorway of at least two pairs of upright stones extending out through the tumulus. Then the number of stones in the sides of the chamber is increased to seven, eight, or nine; and the entrance passage is at right angles to the main axis of the chamber, giving a rude T-shaped form to the whole structure. The number of stones in the roof of the chamber increases with its length. Chambers fifteen to twenty feet long are not uncommon, a length of twenty to thirty feet is rare, a very few attain forty feet. The height was between five and seven feet.

The inner surface of the great stones forming the sides of the chamber is fairly flat. It could have been no easy matter to find in any region a sufficient number of suitable great blocks of the right form. They evidently had some method of splitting large boulders. In some chambers both halves of the same block have been found. These blocks could have been split by heat or by freezing water in a groove or by wooden wedges. But we do not know the exact method. Near the top the blocks often failed to meet exactly. Large holes were filled with bits of wall of small stones and small chinks were stuffed with clay and moss.

It is surprising to find that these smaller and larger chambers were erected without any deep foundation for the upright stones. Many of them have fallen from the heaving of the frost. The monuments were generally adequately protected against this by the thick tumulus.

The tumulus was enlarged proportionately and usually completely covered the chamber. Its height averages ten to fifteen feet, and its diameter over ninety. The culvert-like entrance had to be lengthened accordingly.

But one large chamber did not suffice for successive generations. It was often extended or additions were made so that quite complicated forms occur. In England we find frequently a row or cluster of small chambers. Here the roof is sometimes made of successive layers of stone approaching as they ascended until one slab covered the "false arch." In Brittany we find great diversity as well as complexity of form. In some parts of France the entrance continues the main line of the chamber instead of being at right angles to it. The French have well characterized these as "*Allées couvertes*."

Some of these "gallery chambers" were very large and contained a large number of bodies; sometimes from 40 to 60, in one case 100. The tumulus at Mont St. Michel measures 115 by 58 metres, and forms a veritable hill. Thirty-five thousand cubic metres of stone were employed in the construction of the chamber. Other chambers are from 30 to 50 feet in length. The celebrated chamber at Bagneux, 25 feet long, is composed of fourteen great blocks, of which three form the roof. The great tumulus at *Fontenay-le-Marmion* in Normandy covered eleven chambers in two parallel rows. All the material for these great structures could hardly have been found in the same vicinity. In one case it appears to have been brought from a quarry two miles away. Some large stones, weighing thousands of tons, seem to have been transported many miles.

Some of the latest structures show a certain amount of degeneration. Certain galleries were apparently roofed with timber. We find "dry" masonry, of smaller stones laid in courses but without mortar, alternating with or replacing the great blocks, especially in structures of Æneolithic or Bronze Age. The custom was declining and soon after this disappeared.[1]

The age of these stone monuments can generally be fairly closely determined by the contents, unless these have been removed or destroyed by treasure-hunters, as is often the case. In many cases the objects originally deposited seem to have been few and insignificant. Later, secondary interments were often made in tumuli, but these usually betray their later date by their position above the original chamber or near the side of the mound. We must keep in mind that chambers in the north containing only stone implements may be often of the same age as those farther south containing copper or even bronze, for metal made its way northward only gradually. The custom of building dolmens seems to have persisted later in England than in France. The English round tumuli or barrows belong to the Bronze period. It is not surprising that one country should be more conservative than another, especially if it is somewhat remote.

[1] D: 503.

In Brittany we find the Menhirs or "standing stones," unhewn pillars, regularly accompanying the dolmens. They are by far most abundant in northwestern Europe, but occur elsewhere also. The largest known is the Menhir of Locmariaquer in Morbihan, now fallen and broken. It was almost 21 metres long, and weighed nearly 300,000 kilograms. But specimens are usually much smaller. They seem to characterize the Æneolithic Epoch and the early Bronze Age.

Their meaning is often uncertain. Some of them standing singly were probably erected much later, serving merely to mark boundaries. When associated with dolmens they are probably objects of a religious cult associated with the burial, rather than mere monuments to the dead. They may well be examples of the world-wide pillar-cult. They remained objects or centres of worship until late in historic time. The church had a long and hard battle with their cult. Some of them appear to have been thrown down and churches to have been erected over them. On some of them Christian symbols have been carved. Among the people they are still held in reverence or awe. Whatever may have been their origin, they must have had some religious significance or association.

These pillars may be grouped in circles, cromlechs, or in long radiating rows, alignments. Stone circles occur in the Mediterranean region, in Syria, Upper Egypt, and in India. But circles and alignments belong especially to Brittany, Great Britain, and Scandinavia. The most noteworthy are the three adjacent or connected at Carnac, in Morbihan, extending nearly 4,000 metres, and composed of nearly 3,000 Menhirs. Stonehenge and Avebury in England are almost equally celebrated. They represent the culmination of megalithic development, but are essentially places of worship and assembly rather than of burial, though tumuli may be clustered around them like graves in a churchyard.

The changes in the mode of disposal of the dead are evidently the results of changed views concerning the future life. In early Paleolithic times man buried his dead with the best flint axe in his hand, with his ornaments and a supply of food, and often a quantity of shells brought from a distance and evidently objects of value. The dead man took with him his weapons and all his wealth. For the living to keep back a portion of what belonged to the departed was robbery, which might be avenged by all sorts of evils and plagues; for all this material wealth and ornament was as much needed and as useful there as here. Apparently, though this is anything but certain, the dead were buried at first in Europe, extended at full length, and in the caves not far from the abode of the living.

Soon we find them buried in a crouching position, with knees and hands brought close to the chin. Sometimes we find rows of shells, which may have been attached to cords or bands used to hold the body in this forced position. This mode of burial in a contracted or crouching position (*Hockerbestattung*) was usual in Europe in Neolithic time, but has been discovered in all continents, even in America and Australia. Very different explanations of this peculiar custom have been offered by different observers, *e. g.*, that it saved the labor of digging a larger grave, an excellent economic argument; that the dead was laid in its Mother Earth in the same position which as a fœtus it had maintained in the maternal body, etc., etc. But the predominant thought appears to have been that the spirit remained in, with, or near the body, and that binding the body prevented the spirit from walking and returning to see the survivors. To the same end the most valuable possessions of the dead had been buried with him. This does

ALIGNMENT, CARNAC, BRITTANY

not necessarily argue that there was no affection of the living for the departed, or no belief in their possible helpfulness. But the community generally felt that it was a wise precaution, and generally well to be on the safe side. This belief in the possible return of the dead in their bodily form and presence is still deeply imbedded in our modern minds, ready to spring up as a conscious belief; and the departed are still rarely expected to bring good tidings or benefits.

This mode of burial continued common through upper Paleolithic time; was very common, if not the rule during the Neolithic period in various parts of Europe. Pumpelly found at Anau children, and only children, buried under the floors of the houses, and notices that this custom was general throughout the life of the Kurgan.[1] He gives instances of this custom reported elsewhere. Whether this custom was as wide-spread as the pottery of Anau and Susa seems doubtful. I can find no reports of it. But conditions at Anau seem to have been unusually favorable to the preservation of these perishable remains. It is not impossible that we have here one of the ways in which the fear of the dead may have been gradually dispelled. May we not imagine that one of the first steps

[1] **110**: I, 40.

was the refusal of the mother to allow her dead child to be banished from the house? The evidence is too slight to allow of more than a guess.

As time went on and communities became more closely united leaders must have arisen for whom the people had only affection, in whose wisdom and willingness to help they had full confidence, and who were gratefully remembered as fathers, elders, and wise in counsel, and whose return would have been gladly welcomed. This thought seems to be the foundation of the wide-spread and ancient cult or worship of ancestors. Such cases were certainly common at a somewhat later date, as in the Greek cities, where the bones of the dead leader or hero were guarded as the chief protection of the state. This feeling seems to find expression in the dolmen or house of the dead, with a carefully prepared opening in the door as if inviting the spirit to free egress. Anniversary feasts in honor of the departed were certainly common in ancient days. Close friendship and social relations were cultivated with the departed as knowledge and culture increased.

The Egyptian pyramids and mummies, the graves and older dolmens, seem to testify to a very close and dependent relation between spirit

and body. The spirit hovered around the body
and returned to it, and where the mouldering
bones lay there was the spirit's home. Its life
was a very direct continuance of the life in the
body. Hence also the food and libations and
the rich burial gifts. But toward the close of
the Neolithic period we find the great stone
chamber giving place to a small cyst or vault,
hardly more than a stone coffin, and entirely
underground. At the same time the great stone
circles seem at least to be changing from burial
places to temples or centres of worship. A new
method of disposal of the dead has appeared in
different parts of Europe, in Brittany, for example. Up to this time the body has been of
great importance; it has been scrupulously preserved, and provision made in the grave for the
supply of all bodily needs, though the burial
gifts have steadily diminished in number and
value. Now the body is burned immediately
after death, as if its preservation were no longer
of any importance but a clog and hindrance
from which the spirit was to be set free as soon
as possible. The custom of incineration gains
ground in Europe until in the Bronze Age it is
the rule and inhumation the exception. The
old crass materialistic view has evidently given
place to a far higher and more spiritual concep-

tion of life after death, and probably also before
it. We here catch a fascinating glimpse of the
steady bold working and tendency of the mind
of Neolithic man. It is only a glimpse of one
aspect of his thought and tendency. We lack
the facts to enable us to widen or deepen it.
But it is enough to promise a broad field of
future discoveries.

But one fact leads us to hazard a question.
Not very far in the Bronze Age the first great
wave of Celtic migration seems to have broken
into northern Europe, as the Achæans had already found their way toward or into Greece.
The Celts seem to have had their Vale of Avalon
and Islands of the Blessed, whither the spirits
of the departed migrated. We remember that
when Ulysses went in search of the spirit of
Achilles, and of other comrades in the war before Troy, he sought him in no underground
world, but sailed far across the seas into the
west. Such beliefs, and customs like incineration, are a slow growth, probably far older in
origin than the Indo-European or Aryan migrations, of which some have thought them characteristic. May not this old and wide-spread
belief be merely a continuance of views and
conceptions already held by our Neolithic folk?

We have already noticed the wide distribution of these megalithic structures.[1] They stretch along the shore of the Baltic, North Sea, and Atlantic Ocean down to the Mediterranean. Here they form a band along the south shore. We find them also in Soudan. In Egypt and Greece a far more precocious culture made it possible to replace them by pyramids and "treasure-houses." We find them in Palestine and farther eastward, along the Black Sea, and in India. In Europe they follow the coast lines, and do not seem to have been erected by the dwellers in the valley of the Danube. Their distribution is very similar to that of the great Mediterranean race and its extensions, but they extend far beyond the boundaries of any one tribe or people. They are the expression of a certain thought or conception which spread widely. It might be more correct to say that the general underlying conception was practically universal, but found expression in this form in one area, while in other regions it could not find this expression because conditions were unfavorable.

It is exceedingly difficult to say just where the first dolmens were built. Opinions differ widely. They could have been built only in an area which had a fairly large and settled population

[1] B: II, 102.

who could unite in a large and difficult work, and had the means of carrying it out. The people were agriculturists who possessed no low grade of natural material or mental culture. Many such general considerations lead us to look for their first appearance somewhere in the region east of the Mediterranean, which was evidently the home of many other very ancient forms of culture.[1]

[1] A: I, 423.

CHAPTER VII

NEOLITHIC INDUSTRIES

O UR very hasty glance at different aspects of Neolithic culture has shown its marked diversity in different regions. Its essential and fundamental characteristic was the introduction of tillage and cattle-raising, gradually replacing the mere collecting stage of hunting life, and accompanying a steady growth of independence or control of nature's bounty or stinginess of food supply. This change increased rather than diminished the diversity of culture in different regions. In the rich soil of the loess country and the Danube valley there were genuine farms; in the north cattle and hog-raising probably prevailed, gradually shading over into hunting as one neared the forests. Along the Baltic and the great lakes of Sweden and on all the European rivers fishing was an important source of food. Differences in size, form, and comfort of dwellings tell the same story. In the north we find half-underground huts, probably with shelters of logs or skins in or along the forests. At Grosgartach and in the lake-dwellings and elsewhere we find rectangular houses, veritable homes rather than mere shelters. Primitive man bound the body of his dead with thongs and buried it away in the earth. Then he deposited it in a small stone hut much like his shelter. He enlarged and improved it. Finally the great monument with its circle and alignments seems to have become a temple, and the body, placed in a small cyst or vault, is completely buried, or is burned. These marked changes in burial customs and rites in western and northern, not in eastern or central, Europe, must have been accompanied by changes in the conception of the after life, whether we can trace and interpret them or not.

The same must be said of all industrial products. Every one of them tells a story, if we can understand and interpret it. We are not surprised to find in the late Paleolithic (or early Neolithic) paintings at Cogul women dressed in waist and short skirt not unlike those worn to-day. The dress represented in the idols of southeastern Europe has persisted in the peasant dress of certain isolated regions, especially in Albania, almost or quite into the present.[1] We have noticed the spinning, weav-

[1] B: 310.

MODERN ALBANIAN PEASANTS IN NEOLITHIC GARMENTS

ing, and dyeing of the lake-dwellers, and a similar industry was spread all over Europe. The costume of the Bronze period has been preserved in the oak coffins of Scandinavia.[1] We do not know how much it had changed and improved since Neolithic times. The use of wool had doubtless increased greatly. Our northern Neolithic hunters were probably clad largely in skins and furs.

Two manufactured articles are of especial interest to the archæologist: the stone axes and the pottery. They occur in every settlement. Stone is imperishable, and clay well fired lasts almost as well. They vary according to age, place, fashion, and conditions, and form the foundation for all comparative, "typological" study.[2] Their remains play the same part in archæology as the characteristic fossils, "*Leit-fossilien*," in paleontology, not only determining age but throwing light on the migrations, relations, life, and thought of their makers.

The Neolithic period gained its name from the polished stone implements which then appeared. Paleolithic man had learned by long experience the value of flint as the best material for his tools. He had learned to chip and flake it; first by blows, then by pressure, until the

[1] G: I, 268; J: 90.   [2] B: I, 398.

Solutrean lance-heads or "points" showed a beauty of form and finish unsurpassed by the best craftsmen of any later date. He had learned to give it a fair cutting edge by small "retouches." It seems never to have occurred to him to grind or whet the edge of his tools. If the axe thickened rapidly from the edge and was somewhat like a wedge, it was a good remedy against the brittleness of the flint, its great defect; and he put the more strength into the blow. The extreme hardness of flint made polishing very difficult. Most utensils of daily use were not polished at all. Many of the beautiful daggers, genuine works of art, were finished by a uniform, fine flaking down to the close of the period. Flint implements were not polished in Italy, Greece, Spain, and large parts of eastern Europe;[1] they increase in abundance in Scandinavia and England. Other kinds of less brittle but somewhat softer rock were generally used for polished axes.

During the upper Paleolithic period, especially in the Magdalenian Epoch, daggers, lance-heads, awls, and needles were made of bone. For pointed implements, flint, while sometimes used, was far less suitable, except when the point was very short, as in engraving and carving tools.

[1] H: 20.

These bone implements were scraped into shape and often well smoothed. It seems but a step from smoothing a bone to polishing the edge of an axe, if not of too hard rock. But the chipped flint axe was very good, and they were accustomed to it. Forrer thinks that the change must have been made where flint was scarce and pebbles abundant.[1]

In Scandinavia the kitchen-midden period was followed by an "arctic" culture, so called because of its distribution in the far north. Here we find implements of slate or schist polished only along the edges. This seems like a very natural intermediate stage. We do not know just where those attempts were first made. They may have been made at different points in Asia and Europe and at different times, and thus there may have been several independent centres of discovery and of radiation.

The lake-dwellers used a variety of material; indeed, they seem to have been quite expert practical mineralogists. Characteristic is their use of certain rocks which combined great toughness and hardness, and were thus superior to flint; so chloromelanite, saussurite, nephrite, and jadeite. These minerals are rare, and the implements made of them were small chisel-like

[1] F: Article "Axt."

blades, rarely exceeding an inch in length. They
were usually mounted in a socket of horn fastened into a wooden handle. We shall see that
the source of these minerals is still anything but
clear.

The axe of the kitchen-midden[1] is hardly
more than a disk struck off from a flint nucleus,
with two sides broken off and the top of the
triangular remnant removed. The axe of later
Neolithic time was at first nearly of the shape
of a flattened almond, but gradually changed
and took more of the form of a chisel. The
stages in this process of change are of value in
determining the chronology of the period, and
will be discussed in the next chapter. These
axes were rudely shaped by flaking and then
ground and polished on large flat stones, which
still show the grooves left by the implement as
it was rubbed back and forth. The different
steps in shaping and finishing such axes are well
shown by Hoernes in specimens selected from
the rich collections made at Butmir, Bosnia.

The lake-dwellers followed a different and
improved method. They selected from the bed
of a stream a smooth pebble of somewhat flattened and elongated egg shape. With a flint
flake or saw[2] and sand they cut a groove in the

[1] G: 30; E: 129.   [2] E: Plate 60; A: 506; 96: 330.

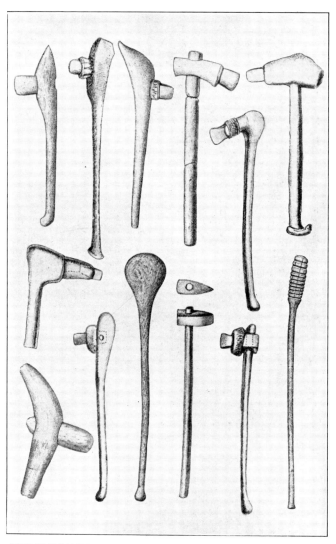

AXES FROM LAKE-DWELLINGS SHOWING ATTACHMENT TO HANDLES

edge, and split the stone by a sharp blow, somewhat as a peanut or almond falls apart. The rounded surface of each half was nearly of the desired form, and only the flat surface required much shaping. A skilful workman now can finish an axe of this kind in half a day.[1]

We cannot trace the variety of axes characteristic of different times, places, and uses. One, which from its resemblance to a shoemaker's last has been called by the Germans the "*Schuhleistenbeil*," demands mention.[2] This is a heavy, thick, clumsy implement, with one end edged or pointed. The lower surface is flat or slightly concave, the upper nearly semi-circular in cross-section. It reminds us somewhat of the grub-hoe or mattock, and probably served a similar purpose — to break up the ground. It is very common in the loess regions of southeastern Europe, but in the more stony soils of the uplands was generally replaced by a pick made of a stout tine of deer's horn. Broader and flatter hoes are found, and stone ploughshares. We must clearly recognize the distinction between the mattock and a somewhat similar but lighter polished concave axe, with sharp transverse cutting edge, used along the Baltic and elsewhere for hollowing out boats. Adze

[1] B: 177.   [2] Figs. 107a, 108.

and mattock are similar in general form, but the carpenter's tool is a much finer instrument than the agricultural implement, and serves a very different purpose.

Bone was still used for pointed tools and weapons. A bundle of sharp pointed ribs found at Robenhausen had probably been used for hackling flax. Horn was used for sockets for the smaller chisels, and for a variety of other purposes. Wooden bowls, scoops, and other articles occur among the remains of the lake-dwellings.

Flint held much the same place in Neolithic industry as iron or steel with us. Its quality varied greatly in different localities. Our Neolithic ancestors had discovered that it worked better when freshly mined than when long exposed and weathered. Hence a mine of flint of the best quality was as valuable as a field of iron ore or a gold mine to-day. The most celebrated source of flint in France was Grand Pressigny, near Tours, Department of Indre-et-Loire.[1] The color and texture of this flint enables us to recognize it wherever found. It was exported as far as Brittany, Normandy, Belgium, and western Switzerland.

At Spiennes, in Belgium, they sunk shafts

[1] A: 355, 629.

sometimes to a depth of forty feet. Here horizontal galleries extended out into the layers of chalk containing the best quality of flint. Similar mines were located at Grimes Graves and at Cissbury, in England.[1] The flint was exported sometimes in blocks, sometimes as half or completely finished implements. Around Grand Pressigny workshops are numerous. But they are by no means limited to the immediate vicinity of the mines. In some localities the manufacture was almost limited to one particular article. Here the product was exported in finished form.

During the Bronze period Halle was a seat of wealth, and the large amount of copper found here suggests that the production of salt had begun here before the close of Neolithic times. Hoernes says that the production of salt at Hallstadt, a source of great wealth and luxury during the earliest Iron Epoch, and of no small extent during the Bronze period, had its beginnings in Neolithic days. The value of salt in trade or barter can hardly be overestimated.

A very small amount of gold, mostly in the form of beads, has been found in the Neolithic monuments of France erected at the very close of this period. Occurring native in small nug-

[1] M: 347.

gets in the beds of streams and rivers of many parts of Europe, its color and malleability must have attracted the notice of the searchers after new material for implements. Large nuggets were found in Spain at a much later date with callais, a mineral resembling turquoise, which occurs from Portugal to Brittany.[1]

Objects of copper were found by Pumpelly at Anau contemporary with the appearance of turbary sheep, about 6000 B. C.[2] It appears in Egypt perhaps 1,000 years later. We find traces of it in the oldest city of Troy (Hissarlik). It may well have entered southeastern Europe by way of Troy, or northward from Greece through the Balkan Peninsula to the Danube valley. A more westerly route lay open through Italy, or the islands west of it, into Spain. Native metallic copper seems to fail in Europe proper, but mines for ore were opened in Tyrol, and probably elsewhere, before the end of the period.

Copper was very useful for ornaments, especially rings, armlets, and bracelets; for pointed objects like needles, pins, awls, and even daggers; to a certain extent for knives and razors. Copper axes were modelled at first after old stone patterns. This metal had one fatal defect, however; it would not hold an edge. Cop-

[1] A: 627; B: 207.   [2] **110**: 50 (chart).

per utensils were beautiful, but generally less useful than similar ones made of stone. They were largely for display and luxury, though this may hardly be true of its use in Egypt and the Orient. In Europe it could not shake the hold of the old, established flint. When the copper ore contained impurities of antimony or zinc, the alloy was harder. Then we find a very small percentage of tin, which slowly increases. There must have been long searching and experimenting before the classical recipe for bronze, ninety per cent copper and ten per cent tin, was established. We cannot well speak of a new copper culture or period. This began with the introduction of the harder and more beautiful, but always rare and expensive bronze. Still the great characteristic of the Bronze Age lay not so much in the introduction of a new metal as in the wider relations, communications, exchange of goods, and knowledge, and freer movements of individuals and peoples, which had brought it about. The discovery of metals, of salt, of minerals, and other materials useful for ornament and of the Baltic amber, was gradually furnishing considerable material which could be readily exchanged for the products of other sometimes distant and more advanced provinces and lands. The centres of distribution were often at some or considerable distance from the sources of the raw material, so especially in the case of flint implements. The location of the seat of manufacture and distribution depends largely on freedom and ease of communication. This leads us to glance at trade and trade-routes during this period.

We must bear in mind that the means of transportation were few and inadequate. The wheeled cart appeared during the Bronze period, but we have no proof of its use earlier. The horse was not yet domesticated in Europe, and did not come into use in the Orient much before 2000 B. C.[1] Cattle may have been used as beasts of burden at an early period, but of this we know nothing. Roads of a certain kind, often probably hardly more than mere trails, almost certainly existed, especially in the neighborhood of the great stone monuments and larger villages. The great bar to free communication was the forest. To avoid this almost impassable barrier the roads and trails seem usually to have kept to the uplands, especially those where the chalk prevented a heavy forest growth. Certain river valleys, like that of the Thames, were heavily forested almost or quite to the shore, and hardly inhabited at this time.

[1] 124: 105.

But when the forest drew back somewhat from the water's edge there was a most attractive place for human settlement. The river bottoms were fertile and easy of cultivation. There was grass for herds, wood for buildings and fuel. The rivers swarmed with fish down to recent times, and there was a great variety and abundance of smaller animal life. Such valleys formed natural routes of trade and migration.[1] We are not surprised to find that the earliest settlers of Sweden made their way from shore to interior along the rivers and lakes, whose shores are dotted with settlements of this age.[2] Déchelette tells us that this was true of the grouping of the Neolithic stations of France in three great provinces in the basins of the Seine, the Garonne, the Rhone, the Saone and the Loire. We remember the lake-dwellers. The valley of the Danube has been the great thoroughfare since the arrival of man in Europe. The great ancient civilizations of Egypt and Chaldea arose in the valleys of the Nile and the Euphrates.

We know that the people of the shell-heaps must have ventured some distance from shore, fishing for cod. The transition from Paleolithic to Neolithic might almost be characterized as a

[1] B: II, 468; D: 511. [2] G: 60.

time of change from a hunting life to one very largely of fishing. Long before this emigrants, probably from Asia Minor, had sailed out into the Mediterranean and settled Crete. Here, before 3000 B. C., a veritable sea-power had arisen carrying on trade with Egypt and the shores of the Ægean. The voyage of the Argonauts, a "much-sung" story and saga in Homer's time, may well have had a historical foundation in expeditions for trade and plunder along the shores of the Black Sea, up its rivers, and extending as far as distant Colchis. Hence the importance of Troy in ancient times and of Constantinople to-day.

Returning to the Baltic region,[1] we find that a cave on the island of Stora Karlso, close to the west shore of Gothland, contained Neolithic deposits nearly three metres thick. In the upper layers there were remains of domestic animals, in the lower only wild forms. This island lies some thirty miles from Oland, just off the east coast of Sweden. Montelius tells us that before the end of the Neolithic period there was communication between Sweden and Finland, as well as with Denmark and Germany; that trade between these regions was active, and that there is reason for thinking

[1] G: 16, 24.

that there was communication between the west coast of Sweden and England. It seems highly probable that boats were creeping along the coast of Spain and France from harbor to harbor, although the evidence is here less clear and compelling.

Our knowledge of Neolithic boats is still very incomplete.[1] Those of the lake-dwellers seem to have been usually hardly more than dug-outs hollowed by fire. One, however, from Lake Châlain (Jura) was about thirty feet long and two and one-half wide, made out of an oak-trunk. Such boats served well for river navigation, but were too shallow and clumsy for the open sea. It would have been a comparatively easy matter to add one or two planks along each side of such a dug-out and thus build up a fairly seaworthy craft. The rock-sculptures of Bohuslan, Sweden, which probably date from early in the Bronze Age, represent boats of fair size carrying as many as thirty men.[2]

The wares exchanged in this trade were limited in material and value. Metals and metallic objects were still unknown, except as copper and gold came in before the end of the period. Still, there were many objects which met a fairly wide demand. We have already seen that

[1] B: II, 483.   [2] G: 127.

different lake-dwellings differed markedly in
their products. Some were almost purely agricultural. In others we find remains of pottery
evidently manufactured on the spot in larger
quantities than the village could use. Much of
this must have been exported along the lake,
perhaps farther. Schliz distinguished at Grosgartach a rude home-made pottery from a finer
ware apparently brought from some centre of
finer and more artistic work. The Neolithic
housewife was probably very proud of this
"china." The finer grades of cloth manufactured at Robenhausen and elsewhere were probably carried far and wide, but it is impossible
to trace it. The flint mined at Grand Pressigny
was transported to greater or less distances, as
well as manufactured at the mouth of the mine.
At the various workshops the implements were
made in great numbers and still more widely
disseminated. This was equally true of flint
regions in other parts of Europe. Stone arm-
rings, mace-heads and other fine articles found
sparsely in northern Europe may well have been
copies of a few articles brought from Italy or
even farther.[1]

The nephrite and jadeite of the lake-dwellings
were long supposed to be imports from eastern

[1] H: 27.

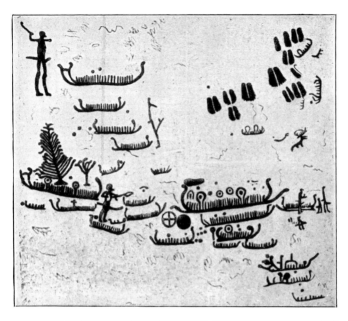

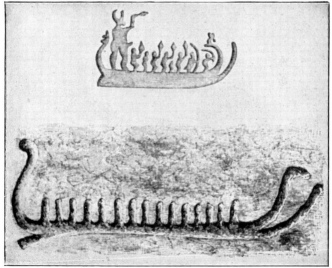

BOATS FROM ROCK CARVINGS IN BOHUSLAN, SWEDEN. (EARLY
BRONZE AGE)

Asia — until it was discovered that the material of many of those implements differed in microscopic structure from the Asiatic, and then were supposed to be of indigenous material. Probably both extreme views are untenable. A certain amount of communication with the Orient is shown by the occurrence of rings made of recent shells of Tridacna or Spondylus in Egypt, throughout the Mediterranean region, in France, and occasionally in middle Europe. The material apparently came from the Red Sea or the Indian Ocean. The same is true of a shell of Meleagrinia found in a hut-foundation in Rivatella, Italy.[1] Ornaments in the form of Mediterranean shells strung as necklaces are not uncommon in France, and occur elsewhere. The Mediterranean lands were in close communication with Egypt and Asia Minor; Spain with Africa, which furnished ivory and carved ostrich egg-shells carried farther north in rare instances. Stone palettes similar to those found in Egyptian graves occur in southern France and elsewhere. More careful search and study will doubtless greatly increase the number of similar illustrations.

Scandinavia was already showing its appreciation of beauty of form and finish, which made

[1] **186**: 168.

its products unsurpassed during the Bronze period. Its marvellous flint daggers and hammer-axes were widely distributed and excite our admiration to-day. But the product which it was later to export to Greece and Italy in payment for the metal and art-treasures of the south was amber, an admirable material for jewelry, easily cut, transparent, of various hues, and taking a brilliant polish. So Homer speaks of a royal necklace, "golden, adorned with amber, like a blazing sun." Far back in Neolithic times we find jars containing large quantities of amber in the form of rude beads. One such hoard contained 4,000 articles, and weighed 17 pounds. The amber was evidently used for necklaces, and was common in the graves of the earlier epochs. It seems to have made its way slowly over North Germany. Amber beads occur very sparingly in the lake-dwellings. During the Bronze period it disappears largely in Scandinavian graves and is here less used for ornaments, but appears in Greece and Italy, where its beauty and possibilities could be properly appreciated. The value of amber in Scandinavia as an article of export rose to such an extent that the inhabitants largely gave up the use of it and exchanged it wholesale for the more attractive and useful metal. During this period there was a regular trade-route between the Baltic and the Mediterranean.

As Hoernes[1] says, it was this new trade which brought with it the close of the Neolithic period in northern Europe. But the change from the age of stone to that of bronze was anything but abrupt or sudden; in fact, it extended over more than 1,000 years. It was apparently not brought about by the invasion of a conquering race, though it was accompanied and followed by marked change and shifting of the population of central Europe. First we find a few copper ornaments and implements stealing into France and southern Europe. Then the metal becomes more abundant as people increase in wealth and can afford luxuries. Then bronze comes in from southeast and south, and very slowly north of the Alps. It meets the current of amber from the north.

Thus the two most beautiful, precious, and desirable materials of the time have come together. Both are easy of transport. A trade which has long been preparing or proceeding on a small scale expands rapidly, perhaps suddenly, and ushers in a new period, which, after all, chiefly carries on or brings into prominence that which had begun or advanced during the preceding age.

[1] B: I, 513.

More interesting and, perhaps, more important than exchange of flint axes and amber is the spread of patterns, methods, influences; of new ideas and stimuli from mind to mind and people to people. A new implement, like the mace-heads and arm-rings, of which we have spoken; a new form of axe or dagger; the form and ornament of pottery; the building of dolmens or the spread of immigration with the accompanying change of cult and thought — all these brought not only economic improvement but growth of mind. Sophus Müller, and Montelius in a less degree, may have been somewhat extreme in their emphasis on the importance of oriental and Mediterranean influences and leadership, but their main thesis was correct.[1] Civilization and culture were far older in the Orient than in Europe, and far more advanced south than north of the Alps. These were the centres of radiation of ideas and stimuli as well as patterns, inventions, and discoveries.

This does not mean that northern Europe was a passive recipient. It accepted and adopted whatever and only what it would, and probably refused many a valuable suggestion. In many cases it improved on the patterns or example of its teacher and inspirer. The art of

[1] H: 49.

polishing stone implements and the use of bronze may not have been indigenous in Scandinavia; but here, as time went on, genuine works of art were produced superior to any in the world, far more artistic than the beautiful technique of the Egyptians. Prehistoric domestic animals were almost certainly introduced from the East. But the lake-dwellers usually improved the breed by intercrossing with forms derived from their own fauna. They increased the list of cultivated plants. The idea or conception passed from tribe to tribe, but the new stimulus did its fermenting work differently, according to the mind or medium into which it fell. There was always readaptation and more or less change. To be a wide borrower and at the same time to usually improve on one's teacher requires something very close to genius, though the originality may be less obtrusive. We have no reason to be ashamed of our Neolithic ancestors.

The result of this exchange of products and ideas will be more apparent during the next period. Trade-routes and lines of communication will then become far more clear and fixed. But it is important to notice that these routes are already opening in all directions, perhaps more numerous because still experimental, tentative, and somewhat vague. The routes of transportation during prehistoric times, as usually in pioneer periods, were mainly along river valleys. Where basins almost or quite touch one another centres of contact and distribution naturally arise. Hence the prosperity of the Department of Saone-et-Loire, in France. A study of any good relief-map of Europe will show the chief routes of trade almost at a glance. The great east-and-west artery is the valley of the Danube, with its tributaries extending far northward, almost touching the headwaters of rivers flowing into the North Sea or Baltic. The westernmost north-and-south route is by sea along the Atlantic coast from Spain to England or Denmark. A second was formed by the Rhone and Rhine, eastward and parallel to the French highlands extending from the Mediterranean to Belgium, broken by the pass of Belfort. A third ran up the valley of the Elbe and down the Moldau to the Danube. This was the most important route in Europe, especially for amber. A fourth, from the Baltic to the Black Sea, followed the Vistula and the Dniester. From ancient times the Black Sea and its tributaries have been the great route of communication between the Ægean and southern Russia as well as parts of the Balkan Peninsula. During the greater part of the Neolithic period it was probably only a sluggish and irregular current of trade which trickled along most of these routes. But it was the beginning and promise of larger and better things, and must not be despised or neglected.

In any study of the industries of this period the manufacture of pottery is of the greatest interest and most fundamental importance. Pottery is to the archæologist what characteristic fossils are to the paleontologist. It is almost indestructible. In its texture, form, and ornament it affords wide scope for individual or tribal skill and invention, and yet over wide areas the general type shows a remarkable unity and persistency. A single sherd may often tell a long and reliable story. The pottery of the Mediterranean basin and of many oriental localities is a fairly sure guide to the age of a long-buried settlement and to the relations of its people with other, often distant regions. The chronology and much of the history of Egypt, Troy, and Crete, and many ancient settlements of Greece and Italy, are based largely on the study of their pottery. It is far more expressive and informing than the average stone or bone implement.

The time is not yet ripe, however, for such deductions from the study of the pottery of northern and middle Europe. A good foundation has been laid, much material gathered which is being built up into a firm system. But in this pioneer work many rash generalizations have been based upon a foundation of facts drawn from a very narrow area, often incompletely understood. Here we must proceed cautiously and can give only a very brief and inadequate outline sketch of the most important results in which we may have a fair degree of confidence and which are needed in our further study.

Pottery appears first in the transition epoch from Paleolithic to Neolithic, at Campigny and in the kitchen-middens. Long before this time there must have been containers for fluids. A concavity in the rock may have been the first reservoir and a mussel-shell the first drinking-cup. Wherever gourds occurred they were doubtless hollowed out and made most convenient jars and dishes. Vessels of bark and wood probably came into use early in the north. Skins of animals tightly sewn with sinew and with well-greased seams formed excellent bottles, still used in the Orient. Where the art of plaiting twigs, splints, or reeds into mats and baskets had been discovered, it was not a long step to coat the inside with clay and dry or

POTTERY FROM NEOLITHIC GRAVES

finally burn it before the fire. The potter's wheel did not come into use until the Bronze period. Pottery had been used in the Orient long before this time. It is found well made and beautifully decorated in the oldest strata at Susa. The art may have been introduced from Asia or lost during the long migration and then reacquired. Here we are still in the dark.

The pottery of northern Europe can be distributed into a few groups or general types, every one of which is wide-spread and fairly distinct, though mixture or combination of types is not uncommon, especially along the boundaries of distribution where two types meet. There is much difference of opinion and discussion concerning details, but general agreement as to fundamentals and essentials.[1]

Intermediate or "hybrid" forms also occur. The classification is hardly natural and is responsible for much confusion and dispute. It can have only temporary and provisional value. These three groups are:

1. Banded pottery, *Céramique rubanée, Bandkeramik.*

2. Corded pottery, *Céramique cordée, Schnurkeramik.*

[1] A: 547; D: 482.

3. Calyciform pottery, *Vases caliciforms, Zo-nenbecher*.

They differ mostly in ornamentation, but often also as distinctly in form.

1. *Banded pottery* occurs all over Europe except northeast of the Oder, perhaps also in Great Britain. Its shape is usually that of a spheroidal gourd with the upper fourth removed; and its system of ornament may have been derived from the system of cords by which the jar was once suspended. Sometimes we find a low neck, rim, or collar around the large mouth. The ornament in what seems to be its most primitive form consists of lines marked in the clay, arranged parallel to one another in bands covering most of the body of the jar. These bands, either broad or narrow, run in a zigzag or saw-tooth pattern horizontally around the base. By doubling each saw-tooth we get a diamond-shaped area. Even this simple ornament admits of a large variety of patterns. But the bands may be curved instead of angular, forming scrolls, meanders, or spirals. Logically, these should represent the latest development of the type. But the spiral may yet prove to be actually older than the angle. The bands may be raised and projecting (Bosnia) or be merely painted on a flat, sometimes burnished,

surface. The incised lines may be plain or filled with a white material (encrusted). The briefest consideration shows that we have here a very generalized type or group of types which made its first appearance in Europe on the lower Danube and then underwent development by simplification or sometimes, perhaps, by increased complexity, as it radiated from this centre, becoming more and more modified as it went westward or northward.

The banded pottery of southwest Germany and the Rhine region is found in dwellings as well as graves, usually accompanied by the mattock or the deer-horn pick, but lance-heads fail. The rectangular houses belonged to people of a settled and quite advanced agriculture. We find cellars, and barns or granaries. The dwellings are single or in groups, sometimes, as at Grosgartach, forming quite a village or town. They are situated by preference on the loess terraces of the streams and rivers, near enough to the water for boat communication. The pottery varies in fineness and beauty according to the size of the dwelling and therefore the wealth of its owner. Social differences, rank, and fashion are appearing in truly modern form.

2. *Corded Pottery.* The most characteristic and, perhaps, culminating form is the Amphora

or flasklike vase with wide neck, which starts abruptly from a globose portion with flat base. Its prototype may have been the leathern flask or bottle. Here the ornament consists of parallel lines arranged in a band or in bands around the neck, but often extending somewhat on to the upper surface of the bulb. The lines look as if made by winding a cord around the neck while the clay was still soft; hence the name of the group. It seems to have been originally a purely northern product, which toward the close of the Neolithic period was carried southward by a distinct movement of population. It is found almost entirely in graves, often accompanied by calyciform cups. Schliz says that it is never found in remains of dwellings. The household pottery was apparently crude and coarse, with no distinctive type of ornament. The carriers of the culture were apparently herdsmen rather than tillers of the soil, and always more or less hunters. Their finest implements were their weapons.

3. *Calyciform Pottery*, *Zonen-* or *Glocken-becher*, has been by some united with Corded Pottery. It has the shape of a goblet or inverted bell with flaring rim and flat base.

The ornament is in circular zones separated by bands of well-polished surface covering the whole outside. It is found in Asia Minor,

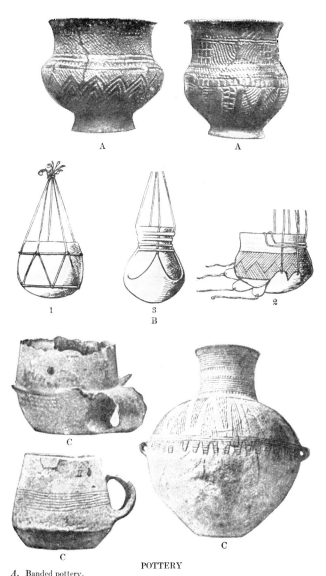

POTTERY

A. Banded pottery.
B. 1. Origin of banded ornament from cords suspending a more or less hemispherical
       vessel derived from the hollow gourd.
    2. Corded ornament derived from suspension of flask (Amphora).
C. Cups and Kugelamphore (globular flask) from Groszgartach.

Egypt, Italy, and in western Europe along the whole zone of megalithic monuments, whence it spread northward and eastward into middle Europe.

The incrusted pottery characterized by incised lines filled with a white material may have had a distinct origin and development, though its technique has often been borrowed and applied to other types. The pottery of the oldest lake-dwellers is crude, coarse, with little or no ornament. Hence it is difficult to connect it with any other type.

Form and shape of pottery are often quite or very persistent. We cannot understand why the base of so many jars was left rounded, or in some old lake-dwellings pointed, when it might easily have been flattened, apparently to good advantage. But even the form, and still more the ornament, changes according to time, place, and fashion; hence these are very useful in tracing periods and cultures and their relations. Where different types meet there is usually more or less change or modification, often difficult to interpret. Our knowledge of European pottery is still small and unsatisfactory, but it has already been of much use in tracing migrations of culture and relations between provinces often widely separated.

CHAPTER VIII

NEOLITHIC CHRONOLOGY

"WE must imagine Europe in upper Paleolithic times again as a terminal region, a great peninsula toward which the human emigrants from the east and from the south came to mingle and to super-pose their cultures. These races took the grand migration routes which had been followed by other waves of animal life before them; they were pressed upon from behind by the increasing populations from the east; they were attracted to western Europe as a fresh and wonderful game country, where food in the forests, in the meadows, and in the streams abounded in un-paralleled profusion. . . . Between the retreat-ing Alpine and Scandinavian glaciers Europe was freely open toward the eastern plains of the Danube, extending to central and southern Asia; on the north, however, along the Baltic, the climate was still too inclement for a wave of human migration, and there is no trace of man along these northern shores until the close of the Upper Paleolithic, nor of any residence of man in the Scandinavian peninsula until the great wave of Neolithic migration established itself in that region." [1]

We must now attempt to determine the succession of these great changes in the climate and face of Europe, and then see if we can fix any dates for some of the changes and for the introduction of new cultures.

In the oscillations of the ice-front marking the final retreat of the Alpine glaciers there were three epochs of advance. Two of these, the Bühl and Gschnitz advances, with the interval of retreat between them, were occupied by the Magdalenian or last epoch of Upper Paleolithic time. The third advance, the Daun Epoch, or perhaps the latter part of the Gschnitz and the first part of the Daun, is represented by the Azilian-Tardenoisian Epoch, a period of transition from Paleolithic to Neolithic time. These changes have been clearly traced by Osborn. [2]

We are most closely concerned with the changes which took place around the Baltic in Denmark and Scandinavia during this postglacial retreat of the ice. Here also we find the same disappearance of the tundra and "barren-ground" fauna already noticed in France, and the appearance of a park-flora of forests interspersed with open glades or meadows. But we

[1] **40**: 279. [2] **40**: 281.

need not be surprised if we find that the retreat of the great Baltic or Scandinavian ice-sheet does not keep step exactly with that of the Alpine.[1]

1. The last ice-sheet had covered most of Scandinavia except the western half of Denmark and, perhaps, the most southern portion of Sweden. But a broad mass of ice covered most of Schleswig, at least the eastern half of Holstein, and a fairly wide zone of land south of and more or less parallel to the south shore of the Baltic. To the eastward and northward a great sea extended to the Arctic Ocean. This earliest stage marked the farthest advance of the ice just before the final retreat.

2. Slowly and gradually the ice retreated until finally it occupied only the mountains of the backbone of Scandinavia. The region of the Baltic Sea and the Gulf of Bothnia, a large part of Sweden and a good portion of Finland were covered by a great sheet of water, the Yoldia Sea, connected by a broad sound at the present Skager Rack with the North Sea and Atlantic, and still opening widely into the Arctic Ocean northeastward. The submerged regions had been greatly depressed, especially in the north. The clays deposited along the shores of the sea, are now raised often to a height of one hundred

[1] D: 465; 49: 540.

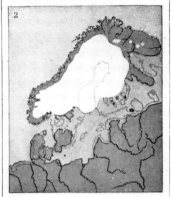
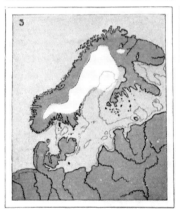

SUCCESSIVE STAGES AND FORMS OF BALTIC SEA

1. Culmination of last advance of ice.
2. Yoldia Sea during retreat of ice.
3. Yoldia Sea at greatest size.
4. Scandinavia during Ancylus Epoch.

(The white represents the ice; dark gray represents the land; light gray the Baltic Sea.)

metres above tide-level. But to the southward the depression was only slightly marked.

It is important to our later study to notice that these clays, which are thick and fine-grained, are composed of thin layers of alternating dark material deposited in fall or winter, and lighter, more sandy, brought down by the spring freshets. The temperature of the sea could hardly have been much above freezing-point, as is shown by the presence of arctic forms of mollusks, like *Yoldia arctica* and *Astarte borealis*. The land-plants of this epoch, the so-called Dryas flora, are dwarf cold tundra forms, now occurring in Spitzbergen, Lapland, and Arctic Russia and Siberia. But certain plants, especially in Sweden, lead us to infer that while the winters were long and severe, the short summers were warm or even hot. This does not surprise us in northern tundra regions. Reindeer still lived in the region. This Yoldia Epoch is our second great postglacial stage. Man had apparently not yet reached Denmark, though some reindeer hunters probably roamed over Germany.

3. Toward the end of the Yoldia Epoch the land rose in southwest Sweden, connecting this country with Denmark and cutting the connection of the remains of the Yoldia Sea with the North Sea. A similar emergence in Finland

completed the change of this sea into a great landlocked body of water called the Ancylus Lake, from the most common and characteristic mollusk, *Ancylus fluviatilis*. The glaciers had shrunken to a narrow band covering the mountains between Norway and Sweden. The climate, while moderating, was still cold. The Arctic flora retreated northward and was followed in Denmark by woods and even forests of willows, aspens, and poplars, entering from the south and southeast. These were followed by pines, especially in the dryer districts, later by alders, coming from the east across Finland, according to Hoops.[1] The Ancylus Epoch forms our third stage. The settlement at Maglemose probably took place toward its close.

4. The elevation and emergence of land so characteristic of the Ancylus Epoch was followed by a depression of this region, especially in its southern portions. That part of the Ancylus Lake corresponding to the Baltic regained broader and deeper connections with the North Sea than it has at present. Hence the waters of the Baltic contained a larger percentage of salt than now. The marine life, *Littorina littorea*, *Tapes*, and others, testifies to a rise in temperature since the Ancylus Epoch. Oaks

[1] 60.

had already begun to crowd out the pines, and will be followed after a time by the beeches loving a soil rich in humus, rather than the sandy barrens occupied by the pines. A similar evidence is furnished by other plants, some of which reached a higher latitude than now. The summer temperature was perhaps $2\frac{1}{2}°$ Cent. higher than at present, an "optimum temperature" for the plant life of this region. This improvement of climate is most marked in northeastern Europe and seems far less noticeable even in Germany. Our fourth stage is marked by a greatly improved climate and the spread of the shell-heaps.

5. A fifth stage ushers in the full Neolithic period. Between the Littorina stage and the genuine Neolithic culture of lake-dwellings and megaliths there is a considerable gap in our knowledge, a period during which agriculture and domestic animals were brought in and utensils and pottery and general conditions were greatly improved.

We may now venture to attempt to gain an absolute chronology of more or less definite dates for the appearance of the cultures which we have noticed. We must clearly recognize that our best results can be only tentative and provisional. A careful study and comparison of the pottery of northern Europe will some day

furnish data for a reliable system. For the sake
of convenience we will begin by attempting. to
set a date for the close, rather than the beginning, of the whole Neolithic period. We have
seen that this was brought about by the introduction of the metal bronze. Copper had come
into use somewhat or considerably earlier, but
it seems hardly worth while to consider it as
characterizing a distinct period. It is rather
the last phase of the Stone Age, when wider
communications and trade were making the
transition to the use of metals like bronze and
iron.

According to Montelius,[1] who is our best authority on chronology, the use of bronze in sufficient quantities to mark the beginning of a new
period took place in different countries at the
dates given in the second column of the following table, the first column showing the date
of the first use of copper:[2]

REGION	YEAR B. C.	
	COPPER	BRONZE
Egypt and Chaldæa..................	5000	3000
Troy, Greece, and Sicily..............	3000	2500
Hungary and Spain...................	3000	2000
Middle Europe and France............	2500	2000
North Germany and Scandinavia.......	2500	1900

[1] 215–218.　　　　　　　　　　　　[2] B: II, 242.

NEOLITHIC CHRONOLOGY   167

These dates mark the beginning of the more or less general use of metals, not the first appearance of a few imported articles. Some authorities would place the beginning of the Bronze period a few centuries earlier, and that of the introduction of copper some 500 years earlier.[1] Forrer dates the beginning of both epochs a little later than Montelius. The date 2000 B. C. would seem to mark the end of the Neolithic period in middle Europe with approximate accuracy.

In attempting to determine the date of the beginning of the Neolithic period we may begin with a remote point of departure for comparison and select the Bühl stage and the beginning of the Magdalenian Epoch. Nuesch made a careful estimate from the deposits at Schweizersbild near Schaffhausen, Switzerland. His method of estimating is described fully by Obermaier.[2] He places the beginning of the Neolithic deposits here at 6000 B. C., and considers 20,000 years as a fair estimate for the time elapsed since the first occupation of this locality by Magdalenian hunters at some time during the Bühl Epoch. Obermaier, summing up the evidence, concludes that the beginning of the Magdalenian Epoch could not have been later than

[1] E: 563.   [2] D: I, 335.

16,000–18,000 B. C., and that it ended not far from 12,000 B. C. Osborn says: "Bühl moraines in Lake Lucerne are estimated as having been deposited between 16,000 and 24,000 years B. C." He also appears to place the Maglemose culture at about 7000 B. C.[1]

We may now turn to the great Scandinavian ice-sheet, whose retreat may have begun somewhat later and proceeded more slowly on account of its more northerly position. Here De Geer has made a report based on a very careful study of the annual layers of deposition formed during the glacial retreat. We have already seen that the material brought down by the spring freshets differs in color and texture from that of late summer and autumn. Hence these annual layers are almost as distinct and as easily counted as the rings in the trunk of a tree. This method promises great accuracy of results, and the thickness and character of the layers and their included organic remains throw much light on the climatic and other conditions under which they were laid down. But even here the length of certain periods of halt in the glacial retreat can be only very roughly approximated. The number of annual layers of deposit in the Swedish Lake Ragunda

[1] 40: 281.

lately drained shows the number of years since the lake was uncovered almost at the end of the retreat of the Scandinavian ice.

Says Sollas: "The Ancylus Lake was in existence at a time when the ice had very nearly, though not quite, accomplished its full retreat, *i. e.*, a little more than 7,000 years ago (the length of post-glacial time); and Baron de Geer, although he has not yet been able to bring the beach of the lake into connection with his system of measurements, thinks, as he has kindly informed me, that its probable date may be 7,500 years counting from the present."[1]

Menzel, in a chart embodying the results of his study of De Geer's work, places the beginning of the retreat of the ice in Germany at 21,000 B. C., the maximum of the Littorina depression and epoch of kitchen-middens at 6000 B. C., full Neolithic at 4500 B. C., beginning of Bronze period 1700 B. C.[2]

Keilhack, basing his study on the silting and dune-formation at Swinepforte, estimates that the time elapsed since the maximum of the Littorina depression down to the present has been about 7,000 years, making the date of the depression about 5000 B. C. He considers his estimate as somewhat more probable than De Geer's.

[1] **49:** 565.   [2] **214.**

Anderson has called attention to the change of position of the earth's axis at different times. When the position of the earth's axis was such as to give most sunlight in Sweden, the midnight sun was above the horizon at Karesuanda, the most northern astronomical station, 62 days. During the time of most unfavorable position it was above the horizon only 38 days, a difference of 24 days. This change should influence climate and vegetation. The period of maximum sunshine, according to this view, was 9,000 years ago, about 7000 B. C., somewhat earlier than the maximum of the Littorina depression. It would tend to give a climatic optimum at nearly the same time as estimated by Menzel.

Steenstrup[1] discovered the succession of forest growths in the peat-bogs or moors of Zealand, north of Copenhagen. In the layers of some of the depressions he found what seemed to be almost a complete record of forest life from the time of the retreat of the glaciers. The upper layers of peat contained remains of trees still flourishing in the surrounding country: alders, birches, and beeches. Then came oaks, and still deeper the pines. Beneath these were aspens, arctic willows, and other plants of the far north. Remains of the reindeer occur in their

[1] C: 225.

lowest layer. The pines hardly, if at all, reached Denmark before the Ancylus Epoch, preceding periods showing only the Dryas flora.

The pines had a hard struggle for life at first. They are dwarfed and their rings of annual growth are very thin, sometimes as many as seventy to the inch of thickness. Still some of these dwarfs attain the very respectable age of 300 to 400 years. Gradually they prospered, and in the upper layers there are trunks more than a metre in diameter. All these facts point to early and long occupation. Steenstrup reckoned the age of the oldest layers of these accumulations at 10,000 to 12,000 years, dating their beginnings therefore at 8000 to 10,000 B. C. Pine was still growing in the neighborhood of the shell-heaps, or the capercailzie or pine partridge would probably not have occurred.

But in the shell-heaps we find only oak charcoal, not pine. This was at least beginning to retreat and give place to the oak. At Maglemose we find pine charcoal but oak pollen grains in layers apparently of the same age as the settlement. Placing the shell-heaps in the early part of the pine epoch would date them as early as 7000 B. C., or even earlier, according to this chronometer. Hence the older writers, who placed the shell-heaps in the pine epoch, dated them considerably farther back than we do now.

Steenstrup's study, a work of genius, is entirely compatible with and probably implies a considerably later date than we used to accept.

The following table shows the dates assigned by different students to Maglemose and the shell-heaps:

	B. C.	B. C.
Obermaier.........	Maglemose, 10,000	Shell-heaps, 8000
Forrer............		Shell-heaps, 8000–6000
Sollas.............	Maglemose, 7,500	
Osborn............	Maglemose, 7,000	
Menzel (Chart)....		Shell-heaps, 6000
Keilhack..........		Shell-heaps, 5000

The shell-heaps and Maglemose hardly seem to differ in age as much as Obermaier thinks; De Geer's study was very careful and certainly demands respectful attention. The tendency toward later dates for these cultures seems to be strong and increasing. If we place Maglemose at 7000 to 7500 B. C., and the shell-heaps 6500 to 6000 we have probably made them as ancient as the facts can well allow. It is better to hold judgment still somewhat in suspense. Even if Obermaier should yet prove to be correct in his apparently extreme dates, it is still evident that the Neolithic period began late

and was of short duration compared with the
millennia in which Paleolithic time was reckoned.

Our records are scanty for the earlier portions
of the more or less than 5,000 years which we
have allowed for the Neolithic period.[1] We
find the shell-heap culture spreading from Denmark into Sweden and Norway. Following
closely, or overlapping it, crossing Norway from
the region of Christiania, we find the Nostvet
and Arctic cultures, perhaps nearly related,
perhaps distinct, but leading over to the genuine
Neolithic Scandinavian culture. Here we find
forms intermediate between the axe and "pick"
of the shell-heap and the axes of later epochs.

We have already described the rude, somewhat triangular axe of the shell-heaps. The
axe of Paleolithic time had had nearly the shape
of an almond. We will compare the pointed end
to the back, and the cutting edge to the edge of
our axe or carpenter's hatchet. The earliest
polished axes of Denmark still retained nearly
the shape of a somewhat long and thin almond.[2]
Their cross-section might be compared to an
ellipse with pointed instead of rounded ends.
This is the "*spitznackiges Beil*" of Müller and
Montelius. It occurs all over Europe and still
farther, while the two following forms have a

[1] 219–221.   [2] 222, 223.

continually more restricted distribution. It is not found in the village settlements or stone graves, and evidently characterizes a period between these and the shell-heaps.

The second form, the *dunn* — or *schmal-nackiges Beil* — may be compared to a long and flattened almond with a small part at the pointed end removed and a narrow strip cut off from each side. The flatter surfaces nearly meet at the end opposite the cutting edge, leaving this end thin. The surfaces have become much more nearly flat, and the cross-section a rectangle with somewhat short ends and slightly curved sides. These belong to the period of the earliest stone graves or still earlier. They could be easily fastened in a wooden handle. This form is very common in Scandinavia.

The third form, the *breit* — or *dick* — *nackiges Beil*, has almost exactly the shape of a thick chisel-blade with broad and thick back opposite the edge, and is rectangular in cross-section. It appears in the later megalithic tombs and the underground stone vaults or cists.

Late in the Neolithic period, usually after the introduction of copper, we find an axe — or "hammer-axe" — shorter and much thicker, somewhat in the shape of a very light stone-mason's hammer, and with a hole for the handle.

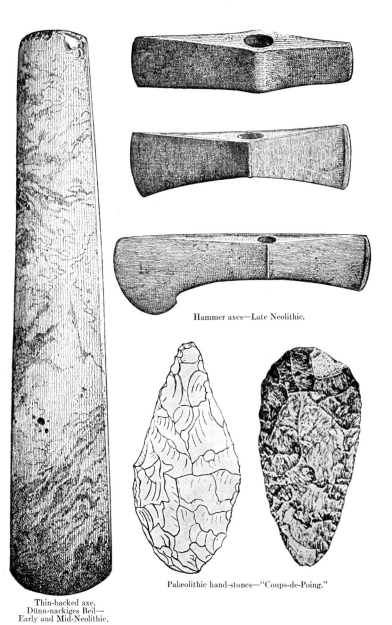

Hammer axes—Late Neolithic.

Palæolithic hand-stones—"Coups-de-Poing."

Thin-backed axe.
Dünn-nackiges Beil—
Early and Mid-Neolithic.

FORMS OF PREHISTORIC AXE

These axes sometimes had two cutting edges, sometimes one edged and the other blunt for hammering. Many of them were exceedingly beautiful in form, design, and finish. But this method of fastening the head to the handle greatly weakened the brittle stone. Many of them were probably merely articles of luxury or adornment. The hole was made by twirling a stick or bone, with plenty of sand, water, and patience.

We have thus in the axes and the megaliths a well-established sequence of forms, but no means of fixing dates except at the beginning and end of the whole period. Apparently there was a long time between the Scandinavian shell-heaps and the fully established Neolithic culture, of which we have practically no records.

Peculiar types of axes (except the mattock), and the megaliths do not occur in the province of the banded pottery, which itself will probably some day give us the clew to a system of chronology. The pottery of Thessaly, Thrace, and certain parts of the Balkan Peninsula is being gradually synchronized with that of Mycenæan and pre-Mycenæan Greece. Important discoveries seem reasonably certain in a not distant future. We can only wait for them with what patience we can assume.

Our real and definite knowledge of the age of the lake-dwellings is hardly better. Hoops tells us that they belong to the Beech period of the Swiss flora. But this period may be much older in Switzerland than in Scandinavia; how much older we do not know. The underground stone burial-cysts of Switzerland look late. The small number of the villages containing no trace of copper and the high grade of household arts and technique in even the oldest of them suggest the same conclusion. Here again it seems dangerous to even conjecture a date.

Montelius, whose opinion on these subjects is certainly of great value, says: "All things considered, I am convinced that the first stone graves were erected here in the north more than 3,000 years before Christ." [1] (It may be safe, therefore, to date them provisionally between 3000 and 4000 B. C.) "The epoch of the dolmens with covered entrance (*Gangräber*) begins about the middle of the third millennium B. C., and the epoch of the stone vaults or cysts (*Steinkisten*) corresponds to the centuries about 2000 B. C."

[1] J: 65.

CHART I. POSTGLACIAL STAGES

RETREAT OF ICE AND CHANGES

SCANDINAVIA	WESTERN AND MIDDLE EUROPE	PARALLELS IN ASIA AND ELSEWHERE[1]	DATE
	1. Aachen Stage.		24,000 (to 40,000) B. C.[2]
Ice-retreats in northern Germany.	Solutrean. Dry and Cold. Steppe and Tundra Fauna.		
Swedish-Finnish Moraines.	2. Bühl Stage. Early Magdalenian. Moist and cold. Tundra.		16,000 (to 24,000) B. C.[3]
Yoldia Period. Dryas Flora.	Middle Magd. Steppe Loess formed.	Susa founded.	
Glaciers in Mountains. Ancylus Lake. Dryas, Birch, Pine Maglemose.	3. Gschnitz Stage. Late Magdalenian.	Anau founded.[5] Neolithic Settlements in Crete.	10,000 B. C.?[4]
Littorina Depression.	4. Daun Stage.		6,000 B. C.?
Optimum Climate.	Azilian-Tard.		(7,000) B. C.?
Oak. Shellheaps.	Campignian.	Sumerians in Babylonia.	
Full Neolithic. Beech.	Full Neolithic.	Predynastic Egyptians. Copper Period.	4,000 (−6,000) B. C.?
Bronze Period.	Bronze Period.	XI–XIII Egyptian Dynasties.	1,900– 2,500 B. C.

[1] See D: 545.   [2] 40: 281, 333, 361; D: 476, 41.   [3] 40: 350, 361.
[4] 40: 281, 449.   [5] 110: I, 50.

CHART II.   CHANGES OF CLIMATE IN DENMARK [1]

1. Arctic climate. Temperature about 8° Cent. Younger
    Yoldia layers, Older Dryas period. Flora: *Dryas
    octopetala, Salix polaris.*
2. Subarctic climate. Temp. 8°–12° Cent. Older Dryas.
    Flora as in 1.
3. Climate becomes moderate, continental. First maximum
    temp. 12°–15° Cent. Birches, poplars, junipers.
4. Climate subarctic. Temp. 8°–12° Cent. Birches.
5. Climate arctic. Temp. 8° Cent. *Salix polaris.*
6. Climate subarctic. Temp. 8°–12°. Younger Dryas period.
7. Temperature moderates. Dry continental climate. *a.*
    Aspen Epoch; *b.* Pine period with oaks beginning to
    appear = Ancylus period.
8. Moderate insular climate. Temp. 15°–17° Cent. Climatic
    optimum. Older Tapes layers, Maximum of Littorina
    depression. Shell-heaps.
9. Temp. 15°–17° Cent. Probably slightly cooler than 8.
    Oak Epoch. Beech begins to appear but is still rare.
    Younger Tapes (Dosinia) layers.
10. Moderate insular climate about 16.1° Cent. Beech Epoch.
    Mya layers.
These climatic changes seem to argue for a comparatively
recent date for the Littorina depression and the shell-heaps.

[1] See 214.   Chart 219., cf. 210.

CHAPTER IX

NEOLITHIC PEOPLES AND THEIR MIGRATIONS

THE study of history without a thorough knowledge of geography is almost as futile as the hope of interpreting the structure of the ape without thinking of his arboreal life.[1] Contour lines are of vast, often dominant, importance in the life of every nation. John Bull has been moulded, if not made, by his island. Italy could never be safe until its boundary followed the crest of the Alps. Great mountain chains mark limits, and river valleys are thoroughfares. Whoever holds Constantinople controls the trade of a boundless area. If this is true to-day, it must have been far more important in prehistoric times, when man had only begun to gain a certain degree of independence or mastery of nature. Culture was then very largely determined by position and routes of communication. The Alps and Pyrenees formed a long, impassable barrier between northern and southern Europe, broken only by the Rhone valley; and northern Europe was split into an eastern or middle and a western province

[1] 240, 241.

by the Juras, the Vosges, and the forested Ardennes. Then, as now, the Pass of Belfort was the narrow opening, and Belgium, always the battle-ground of nations, the great thoroughfare between middle Europe and France. From the south, and to a certain degree from the west, middle Europe was not easy of access. But to the eastward there are few or no natural boundaries as it goes over into the great Russian plain, of which North Germany is practically a westward projection. We might possibly go farther and accept literally the somewhat exaggerated statement that all Europe is only a peninsula of Asia.

Osborn has called attention to the fact that from Paleolithic to Neolithic time Europe gave rise to no new races.[1] The immigrants entered their new home with all their physical and mental characters already fixed or determined. The routes of migration of the successive waves of lower Paleolithic immigrants are still unknown. Remains of Chellean and Acheulean cultures are rich and widely distributed everywhere around the Mediterranean, especially in northern Africa, at this time well watered. The entrance of Neanderthal man into Europe may well have been from this direction.

[1] 242.

The Cro-Magnon race very probably came along the northern or southern shores of the Mediterranean, and then pushed northward into France; though the evidence is far from compelling. The race is evidently Asiatic in its physical characters, reminding us of tribes still living along the Himalayas, most strikingly of the Sikhs. If they entered from the south, northern Africa was a station on their march, not their original home. The Solutrean culture may have been brought by the Brünn people, who probably came through Hungary and up the Danube, but its origin and route of migration is still very obscure. Breuil's arguments for the migration of Magdalenian culture from Poland across Europe are very strong, and his view seems to accord well with the facts, though Osborn seems to lean toward a somewhat different interpretation.[1] The broad-headed people of Furfooz and Grenelle apparently came by the central European route. The only race showing any Negroid characters is that of Grimaldi, apparently accompanying the Cro-Magnons, few in number and having little or no influence on the population of Europe. Evidently the Mediterranean region was far more precocious than northern Europe, and the genuine Mediter-

[1] 243.

ranean race may have arrived here bringing the Neolithic culture almost or quite as early as the beginning of the Upper Paleolithic Epoch in France.

Sergi is of the opinion, though he does not press it, that the Mediterranean race originated in Africa, perhaps in the region of the great lakes, and that its most primitive representatives of to-day are the Hamitic peoples along the southern shore of the Mediterranean.[1] His definition of the race is based less upon mere breadth and length of skull than upon contours and form and development of regions. It was a work of observation, insight, and genius, and was a landmark in the progress of the science of anthropology.

The area of distribution of the race takes the form of a Y, the arms following the north and south shores of the Mediterranean while the stem or lower portion extends through Asia Minor. It includes the Hamitic peoples, also the Pelasgi and the Hittites, but leaves out the Semites.

Huxley had described the distribution of his Melanochrooi, or dark Europeans, very similarly, except that in his group the stem of the Y lay farther south and extended into Arabia. In lo-

[1] 244: 39–43.

cating the origin of the Mediterranean race in
Africa, Sergi was doubtless influenced by the
opinion of Darwin and others that man's birth-
place was in Africa.   Nearly all paleontologists
to-day favor the Asiatic origin; and the stem of
the Y stretching eastward toward Asia Minor
or Arabia points to a possible or probable primitive route of migration.   The Asiatic cradle is
really in better accord with Sergi's theory, and
meets some objections or difficulties better, than
the African.

We vaguely located this Asiatic cradle somewhere westward or northwestward of the great
plateau of Thibet.   We may call it the Iranian
plateau, using the term in the broadest possible
sense, including Afghanistan and perhaps western Turkestan: a great area extending more than
1000 miles from northwest to southeast, where
it sinks into the valley of the Euphrates.   We
found a branch of the great Negroid race starting very early from this region and migrating
westward past Arabia into Africa.   This was
an easy line of least resistance through regions
where the moist, cooler climate of the glacial
period brought only blessing instead of calamity
and curse.   The Hamitic and Semitic peoples
naturally followed the same route, travelling as
one people or nearly together, if the relations

between the languages are as fundamental and close as some good authorities think. The Semites settled in Arabia, while the Hamites went on westward and found a home along the southern shore of the Mediterranean. We do not know when this migration took place.

This route was easy and wide, and led into a broad, favored continent. It would not be surprising if for a very long time most of the travel went this way. We may venture to guess that Neanderthal man may have followed it long before the beginning of the Hamitic-Semitic migrations, but this is only a guess. While rich, well-watered, and probably park-like in its flora during the moist climate of the glacial epochs, it was sure to degenerate into desert as the climate became warmer and dryer; as the Sahara Desert is dotted with the remains of Paleolithic settlements where the explorer to-day is in danger of perishing from thirst. Any traveller by this southern route must pass through Italy or Spain before reaching northern Europe.

A second great western route must have begun very early to compete with the African. This led along the curve of the mountain ranges of Persia and Armenia, with Breasted's fertile crescent at their base, up the valley of the Euphrates

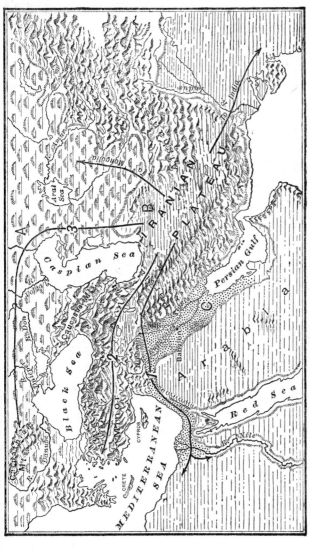

F. B. Loomis, del.

MIGRATIONS OF PEOPLES

1. The southernmost route to the Mediterranean and Africa. The middle part of this route follows roughly Breasted's "Fertile Crescent," as shown in his History of the Ancient World, around the headwaters of the Euphrates and Tigris. 2. Middle route through Asia Minor. 3. Northern route around Caspian Sea to Carpathians. *A.* Grass-lands and steppe. *B.* Iranian Plateau (central portion). *C.* Valley of Mesopotamia.

and elsewhere into Asia Minor. This route
continued in use as a great thoroughfare for
migrating peoples and invading armies through
historic times. Xenophon and his 10,000 explored it. It is surrounded on three sides by
water, although mountain chains cut off the
influence of the sea to some extent. It is a
plateau of glade and forest, though the forests
have now largely disappeared. It has the
features of a semitropical climate; here the flora
of northern and southern provinces meet and
overlap. One great characteristic of the region
is the abundance and variety of its fruit-trees.
It was apparently the original home of apricot,
peach, fig, and orange, as well as of other fruits
introduced into Italy from this region by the
Romans. The vine is luxurious. Somewhere
along the line of this great thoroughfare the wild
olive was domesticated, improved, and transformed. Oaks, walnuts, chestnuts, and many
smaller growths furnish a variety of nuts. The
open glades tempted to agriculture and furnished
no small contributions of grain to Rome.
Though suffering from dessication, it may yet
again become the garden of the world.

When once a wave of westward migration had
entered Asia Minor it was walled in on the
north and south by mountain and sea. There

were no by-roads. Crowded and pressed from behind, it could not stop until they reached the shores of the Ægean Sea.

Here there were two possible outlets. One was by sea, using as stations the islands with which the sea is dotted and leading to Crete and to Greece. Crete, according to Evans, was settled some 14,000 years ago, and is on the whole less easily reached by short voyages than Attica. A second outlet led across the Hellespont and around the Ægean Sea into Greece, or still farther northward and westward around the Adriatic and down into Italy. We might add still a third fork of this great highway running northward to the Danube. When we remember how Neolithic settlements in northern Europe clustered around the lakes and dotted the river valleys, the primitive minor routes of communication, how early islands like Crete in the south and Gothland in the Baltic were settled, we can imagine the importance of a city — or even a village — like Troy even in prehistoric times. Here a sea route running east and west crossed a great land route running north and south. Here was a point of exchange, trade, and transshipment — if we may use the word. We do not wonder that before the close of the Neolithic period, and perhaps far earlier, patterns and influences were radiating through the Balkan region, far up the Danube, and we know not how far into Russia.

It is hardly an exaggeration to say that Greece, and Italy to a less extent, were in climate and many other features bits of Asia Minor, almost shut off from northern Europe by the great Alpine barrier. The two regions were entered by different routes, each of which had left its mark on its travellers. Immigrants seeped into Italy and Greece through broken and rough mountain regions. Great invasions were difficult or impossible. They were sunny, smiling lands compared with the grim and dreary north. Men living in this milder climate did not need to be gross eaters. They lived from the fruits of their orchards to a far larger extent. Nuts were in early times almost a surrogate for grain. The olive furnished a delicious oil, and the grapes wine. The butter and cheese of northern Europe were neither needed nor desired.[1] Most of these habits, tastes, and desires had become fixed during the march through Asia Minor.

The peoples which gradually went westward from the Iranian plateau through Asia Minor, across or around the Ægean Sea into Greece and Italy and Spain, generally found a very similar

[1] 245.

environment from beginning to end of their long journey. There was little in food, climate, or conditions to compel or stimulate change. Everything tended to more firmly fix in their structure the already long-inherited characters of their Iranian ancestors. These characteristics thus fixed have become stable and persistent, and have remained so in modern times in spite of repeated invasions and infusions of northern blood. We are perhaps justified in speaking of a Mediterranean race.

It seems strange that Sergi should find traces of his Mediterranean race in Russia. Did these find their way so far northward directly from the Mediterranean area or are they merely sporadic groups more resistant to modifying influences; or are they perhaps groups which have separated from the westward migration at the Hellespont and turned northward? The Nordic peoples of Europe are perhaps after all not so far from their Mediterranean cousins. The Mediterranean race still holds its own around the Mediterranean. In France its blood is much mixed and greatly diluted with later infusions. In England it has generally been almost completely swamped by Aryan invasions.

Neither of the two routes already sketched leads directly into middle or northern Europe.

The trend in both is toward the Mediterranean. We must now consider the third and last route, which is of chief interest to us. We have already seen that the Black Sea prevented all migrations northward from Asia Minor except at the Hellespont. Eastward from the Black Sea lies the Caspian, probably much larger in glacial times. The two seas are separated by the forbidding, almost unbroken, mountain barrier of the Caucasus; but a narrow passage at each end is left. East of the Caspian Sea must lie the point where a more northerly westward route diverges from the road through Asia Minor. Our third route starts, therefore, from the northern edge of the Iranian plateau, perhaps mostly from Turkestan, and runs westward north of the great barrier of seas and mountains just described. It follows the great steppe or prairie which stretches through southern Siberia and Russia into Hungary. Its western portion lies along the valley of the lower Danube, the great east and west artery of communication and migration through Europe. It lies farther north than any other great route, and leads over steppe instead of through forest. As the Arabia-Africa route was the first to be traversed, this may well have been the last. Furthermore, the route through Asia Minor, ending in a sort of *cul de sac*, may easily have become well inhabited and hence less open before the Neolithic period had begun in northern Europe.

It was by no means the most attractive route. It offered far less to people in the collecting stage than the well-watered parklands of Asia Minor. The steppe offers to the hunter few means of concealment or approach to the game. The animals are swift and wary. In any migration of peoples toward the frontier, the hunters lead the advance and spread out like an army of scouts. Every river which crossed the steppe would offer to them a tempting by-road leading off into the forests of Siberia or Russia. How deeply they would penetrate into the primeval forest or away from the river valleys is still a question. Very likely they would find their best hunting-grounds not very far from the northern edge of the steppe, where the forest is less dense. This question we cannot yet answer. But most of European Russia is well watered, and here these hunters would find themselves at home. The main route of the steppe would be left for a very different population. The piedmont zone of grasslands in Turkestan was an ideal land for primitive agriculturists practising a hoe-culture, as at Anau. The northern edge of this steppe zone, where it joined the forest, may have been equally favorable.

But the piedmont zone and the river banks of the steppe must have been occupied by agriculturists before 10,000 B. C., probably much earlier. Pumpelly's explorations seem to warrant this view. Alongside of agriculture, but at a somewhat later date, sheep-herding and cattle-raising were practised. But the nomad of these days was a less dangerous neighbor than at later times because the horse had not yet been domesticated. During these post-glacial times he would be less dangerous here than farther south around Arabia, when the dryness which finally produced the Arabian desert was making itself felt, burning up the pastures and leaving only the choice between starvation and migration in mass. Again comparing this migration with the pioneer movements of peoples in historic times, we have good reason to believe that the sheep-herders and cattle men — and they were probably both at the same time — advanced faster than the agriculturists, who were more bound to the soil. Between herdsmen and farmers there were almost certainly many intermediate grades. We may be fairly confident, therefore, that the movement or tide along this route did not take the form of a procession marching in lock-step, but of a series of waves, generally with hunters in front and along the forest flank, herdsmen in the middle, and farmers bringing up the rear and making permanent settlements at favored spots.

Hunters had been spreading northward at least as early as the beginning of Upper Paleolithic times. Farming on the lowest grades of agriculture is essentially Neolithic. A town or village had risen at Susa 20,000 years ago. Neolithic civilization probably reached Crete nearly or quite 15,000 years ago. Small Sumerian cities were being founded in southern Babylonia at or before 5000 B. C. Population was increasing in density in the Iranian plateau, as almost every mountain region with its healthy atmosphere and low death-rate quickly becomes overpopulated. Our pioneer column was continually pressed forward by new recruits from the rear as well as by its natural increase. We have practically no records of the march. But our sketch is no mere invention of fancy. It applies to every great migration of peoples extending over centuries or millennia. The last illustration was the great westward movement in America beginning a century or two ago, and still far from completed.

The Hungarian plain is the last extension of

the great south Russian steppe far into Europe.
West of this anything like nomadic life was
practically impossible. Here our pioneers scattered and followed the river valleys, settling
more or less permanently the loess deposits as
farmers, but on less favorable soils devoting
themselves more largely to cattle-raising. The
latter form of life seems to have been more
common on the great North German plain,
though accompanied by much hunting, a genuine
pioneer life.

We may now turn to Europe and consider
the distribution of its races and peoples.

Of the route of migration of the Neanderthal
race we have no sure knowledge. The wide and
rich distribution of ancient Paleolithic implements in Egypt and northern Africa tempts us
to guess that it represents a very early migration along the Arabian route after the negroids
and before the Hamites and Semites. We have
glanced at the origin of the Cro-Magnon people, and have discovered our uncertainty. The
Tardenoisian culture, with its pygmy flints, is
exceedingly wide-spread,[1] and seems to have
started in Europe in the Mediterranean region,
arriving from still farther east. We are tempted

[1] **40** : 465.

to guess that the great bulk of westward migrations in Paleolithic times followed the southern, Arabian, route, but there were probably exceptions.

Coming down to Neolithic times we find the Hamitic peoples in Africa, apparently representing the first wave in the migration of the Mediterranean race. It may well have arrived at its present home long before the beginning of the Neolithic period. It had followed the southern route. Peoples physically and racially closely akin to the Hamites followed, probably in successive waves. The Tardenoisian people, if their culture was carried by a distinct people, may represent an early wave. The bulk of the population of Greece, Italy, and Spain followed, but migration seems to shift gradually from the Arabian route to that through Asia Minor, as the zone of most favorable climatic conditions moved slowly northward. Before the close of the Neolithic period the relations between Greece, Crete, and western Asia Minor have become so marked and close that they almost represent one culture and people.

The Mediterranean race, thus established in Europe, spread northward. It could not cross the Alpine barrier. It followed the Rhone valley and the Atlantic coast, and furnished the

NEOLITHIC PEOPLES

basic population in France and Great Britain, though here frequently crowded back into corners or submerged by later invasions, peaceful or otherwise. It furnished the great link or means of communication between the Mediterranean basin and the far north of Europe. Schliz has some reason for calling these megalith people largely traders.

In a cave near Furfooz, Belgium, there were found crania, probably of Azilian-Tardenoisian time, noticeably distinct from those of the long-headed or dolichocephalic Paleolithic peoples in being short — and broad-headed, brachycephalic.[1] Brachycephalic crania, perhaps early Neolithic, were also found at Grenelle near Paris. We remember their occurrence in the shell-heaps at Mugem, Portugal. Similar crania were found of about the same age at Ofnet, Bavaria, on a tributary of the Danube.

Somewhat later we find broad-headed people occupying the higher lands of southeastern France, the *Massif*, Juras and Vosges, forming thus a north-and-south zone separating France from middle Europe. They seem later to have gradually spread westward, somewhat irregularly, and to have mingled with the Mediterranean peoples of France.

[1] 268–272 a.

The relation of these "Protobrachycephals" to the great Alpine race, most of which arrived later, is still a matter of discussion, and the whole problem of the brachycephalic peoples bristles with interesting questions. They seem to have originated in the mountain regions of western Asia, possibly in or near the Armenian highlands, though this has been disputed.[1] It looks as if they came originally from a region bordering on or overhanging the steppe route and came into Europe by way of the valley of the Danube. There were certainly several if not many waves of brachycephalic migrations into Europe, of which this was the first. Other waves may have come from different parts of a great area, and hence show modifications of type. Everywhere the Neolithic brachycephals seem to inhabit mountainous or rough country, perhaps because of preference, perhaps because as they gradually made their way they found these regions unoccupied. They seem to be an unassuming, unpretentious, peaceable, exceedingly persistent and enduring stock, which has held on its way with remarkable pertinacity. Some still maintain that brachycephaly is everywhere largely an adaptation to conditions and habits of life.[2] The rough country, generally heavily for-

[1] 272.   [2] B: I, 302.

ested, and well populated with this quiet but firm and solid people, greatly hindered free communication between France and central Europe.

No human remains have been found in the Danish kitchen-middens, which may well have been heaped up by broad-heads from Belgium but apparently mingled with eastern immigrants who brought with them the domesticated dog not found at Mugem. They left their axes and picks in Sweden and across into Norway. Behind them came people bearing the Nostvet culture.[1] Our knowledge of Russian prehistory is still very scanty. But we find here a variety of cultures, such as we should expect from a confusion of hunting tribes far from their original home much broken up and remingled during the long migration. We find in Poland the remains of a culture akin in its carvings to the Magdalenian culture of western Europe.

It would hardly have crossed Europe from the west. Breuil[2] seems to consider it as the station from whence it was carried to France. The question is exceedingly interesting and important, but is one to which we can give no sure answer. The carved bone implements are certainly to be found in Poland and to the northward.

[1] 220.   [2] 220.

Behind these bits and wrecks of tribes and cultures, for they were hardly more, came the first great recognizable body of Nordic peoples, probably also in successive waves mingling on this northern coast toward which they had been drawn by the climatic optimum. Kossina,[1] who has given an excellent account of these early northern migrations, speaks of them as *Urfinnen* and *Urgermanen*, primitive Finns and Germans. *Urskandinavier*, primitive Scandinavians, would seem to be a more appropriate name. For the centre of the least mixed blood of this group is to be found in the Scandinavian peninsula.

These Scandinavian representatives of the so-called Nordic race or stock are characterized by tall stature, blond complexion, light hair, blue eyes, and long head and face. Their origin is still a matter of much discussion. Kossina and others derive them from Cro-Magnon people, following the reindeer in its migration north-eastward from France at or toward the end of the Magdalenian epoch. Some suggest that the Cro-Magnon people were also blonds. If this were so they formed a marked exception to the color of Paleolithic stocks coming from and through southern regions. The possibility can-

[1] 220.

not be denied. But, if the Cro-Magnons were light-colored, they have left no traces of this in their descendants at Perigeux and elsewhere. The face of the Cro-Magnon was short and broad, that of the Scandinavian long and narrow. It might have changed but has not done so at Perigeux. The Cro-Magnon race was already declining in physique and numbers during the Magdalenian. Even if all migrated, could they have furnished enough descendants to give rise to the Scandinavian population? It seems to me far more probable that the Scandinavians were hunters or partially herdsmen, who had wandered by the steppe route through the forests or along their edge, and had lost the dark pigmentation in the northern climate. This has been noticed, perhaps to a less extent among Asiatic steppe-dwellers.

The study of prehistoric anthropology in Russia, a vast territory, is still in its infancy. We have touched upon only one or two of the questions concerning this so-called Nordic race, which is probably hardly more than a name for a mixture of peoples.[1] We must not forget that even in Scandinavia we find traces of a very early immigration of short-headed people.[2] We still know little concerning life in North

[1] B: I, 334–337, 307.　　　　[2] 246.

Germany during the Neolithic period. It was probably what we should call pioneer life, where hunting and cattle-raising and a rude tillage combined to furnish support.

We must now turn to the valley of the Danube. Here we find a population characterized by similar ground form of skull, although according to Schliz[1] showing two fairly distinct varieties, a longer and a shorter cranium. Probably this population arrived in several successive waves. Its culture is evidently homogeneous. They are agriculturists forming fixed and permanent settlements, practising farming of a high grade. The characteristic implement is the mattock. Daggers and lance-heads are rare, or fail. They were a peaceful folk settling by preference, though not exclusively, in the loess districts, as at Grosgartach. We find, as we had every reason to expect, that northern Germany and Scandinavia were peopled by a pioneer folk not yet completely agricultural. The Danube people represent the farmers of the steppe whose migration probably went on more slowly and gradually, and who always remained more homogeneous physically and culturally. They may, or may not, have reached the Danube valley as early as the Germans and Scandinavians arrived

[1] 250: 202, 206.

at the Baltic, for they had far less distance to march. They spread out westward and north-ward. Here we trace them by their pottery. Starting from Hungary and the surrounding re-gions we find them in Moravia, Bohemia, Silesia, across south and middle Germany as far as the Rhine. We have already noticed that the banded pottery covered all this region, while the home of the corded pottery was North Germany.

But, while the form of the banded pottery is quite constant, the ornament varies greatly. We find the plain, often rude, saw-tooth pattern, the meander and scroll, the spiral-painted pot-tery—sometimes in the southeast plant patterns, perhaps introduced. I regret that I cannot find any clear or definite theory as to the exact rela-tions of any of this pottery to that of Anau or Susa. The greatest variety, as well as the most complex patterns, seem to occur in most southeasterly regions, which, at least in later Neolithic times, were much under the influ-ence of the Ægean culture, just as western Europe borrowed from Italy and Spain.

Here there was evidently a great and very complex mixture of cultures, and probably of peoples all of one great primitive stock, shown least modified in the Mediterranean race, here more influenced, changed, and varied by steppe climate and conditions, and more or less admixture.

Along the Swiss lakes we find the lake-dwellers. The few human remains from the earliest lake-dwellings are all brachycephalic — short-heads. Then in the period when copper was beginning to come in we find long-heads arriving in greater numbers, but the short-heads regain their superiority during the Bronze period. The weight of evidence seems to favor the view that these settlers did not come from the zone of "proto-brachycephals" inhabiting eastern France, but represent a new immigration from the east, and, according to Schliz, founded fortified settlements on the heights of Baden, Wurtemberg, and along the valley of the Rhine as far as Cologne.[1] We have seen that the pottery of these earliest immigrants was crude and almost or quite without definite ornament.

Northern and central Europe seem to have been settled mainly or almost entirely directly from the east, along western Russia and the Danube valley. But, especially toward the close of the period, people from the megalithic zone seem to have penetrated much farther southward into Germany than their monuments would prove. Schliz thinks that he has recog-

[1] 250: 205.

nized their skulls as well as calyciform pottery over a wide region. Their presence seems fairly clear, but whether they were comparatively very few in number, or fairly numerous, is still uncertain.

There seems to be good reason for believing that in late Paleolithic time the population of middle Europe north of the Alps was very sparse and the Baltic region hardly inhabited. A hunting population without domestic animals except the dog pressed northward through Russia in waves and fragments, and along the Baltic mingled with a strain coming from the west, probably broad-heads from Belgium. The great Scandinavian and North German peoples followed with a frontier culture, a combination of hunting, fishing, cattle-raising, and agriculture mingled in proportions varying according to time and place. Their exact route of migration from the region of the steppes must yet be traced. But the weight of evidence favors an eastern origin. At a time probably not so very far from their arrival in the north, agriculturists — we might safely speak of them as farmers — were coming into the Danube valley and spreading along its tributaries. Apparently somewhat or considerably later the lake-dwellers appear along the northern piedmont zone of the Alps as broad-heads, marking the arrival of the advance guard of the great Alpine race of to-day. But here again our certainty is not as firm as we could wish. They extend northward toward and along the Rhine valley. The close of the period is marked by the southward spread of peoples from northern Germany crowding back the farmers characterized by the banded pottery. This movement is augmented somewhat, perhaps very little, by recruits from the megalithic zone of northwestern Europe and Denmark. All these people are closing in on central or middle western Europe. In the Rhine valley along the middle of the course of the river we find a region of mingling or overlapping cultures which have not yet been satisfactorily disentangled.

We have spoken of them as pioneers. It was a time and place of pioneer, frontier life. And frontier men and life have their peculiar physical, cultural, mental, and temperamental characteristics, almost apart from time and place. The people have something, at least, in common with the great American westward migrations and frontiersmen of a far later date. We have the successive waves of hunters, herdsmen, and farmers often overlapping or mingling. We have a grand mixing of peoples and cultures, if not

of races. Many a fine art or technique is left
behind. Life is rude, hard, vigorous, vital, joy-
ous. It was so yesterday, it was probably so
millennia ago. For the stratum of frontiersman
and barbarian — not to say savage — lies just
below the surface in us all, and a scratch ex-
poses it. This was a period of vitality, hope,
and promise.

CHAPTER X

NEOLITHIC RELIGION

MAN'S ancestors, as we have seen, owed their progress to their training, policing, and harassing by stronger and better-armed competitors. The earliest vertebrates developed a notochordal rod of cartilage, and then a backbone, by the habit of swimming forced upon them by the mollusks and crustacea which held the rich feeding-grounds of the ocean bottom along the shores. In early Paleozoic time the sharks crowded the ganoids in successive waves toward and into fresh water, until finally some crawled out on the shore as amphibia.

Land life and air-breathing gave the possibility of warm blood and high development of brain, and a strong tendency toward viviparous and finally intrauterine development of the embryo. Reptiles harassed mammals into the attainment of a certain amount of wariness and intelligence. The comparatively weak Primates were kept in the trees and forced to develop hand and brain by the fierce and well-armed

Carnivora. Only a "saving remnant" has progressed, and these mostly under stern and strenuous pressure. The "aspiring" ape exists only in our imagination.

The apes had become accustomed to life in the trees, and found it safe and comfortable. A change of climate compelled those dwelling farthest north to seek their living on the ground. Most of them fled southward, many became extinct, a few came down and adapted themselves to the new mode of life. Nature was in no sense a "fairy god-mother" to them, but a stern, harsh disciplinarian whose method of education was "not a word and a blow and the blow first, but the blow without the word, leaving the pupil to find out why his ears had been boxed"[1]; and nature's cuffs were frequently fatal. The pupil had to learn by others' experience. Paleolithic man lived in France poorly armed and ill-protected against a threatening climate steadily changing for the worse. Food may have been abundant, but enemies hunting for him were also numerous. He was compelled to be keen, watchful, prying, wary; to discover distant danger, and to notice every trace of its approach. He learned the habits and behavior of animals, and the ways of things — an excel-

[1] **290**: 85.

lent course of study. He had to rely on his wits, and they were none too keen or many.

Some things he could understand: he learned to avoid or to ward off many dangers. Others seemed altogether beyond his understanding or control. Here he could only wonder; but the wise old Greeks knew that wonder was the mother of wisdom. He wondered at storm, lightning, hail, and flood; at disease and death, and a hundred other things. He sat in the mouth of his cave and watched that strange creature fire devouring the wood and sending smoke and sparks skyward. He thought a very little in a dull, stupid way, dozed and dreamed and awaked to wonder again. Or he saw fire raging through the forest and fled for his life. But it was warming and fascinating, and somehow akin to himself. Did it not devour wood and lap up water on the hearth?

He seems to have come to feel rather than recognize that he was surrounded by invisible powers, in some respects like himself but vastly more powerful, who knew what he was doing, and who would hurt him if he did certain things and might help him if he did others. Certain places were to be strictly avoided, certain objects must not be touched, certain things must never be done, or could be permitted only at certain times. They were taboo. He has started on a long journey of exploration, experiment, and discovery.

How had he come to believe this? Largely through hard experience of nature's buffets, whenever he acted contrary to this hypothesis or feeling. His religion was largely one of fear fitted for a savage mind, though not without a mingling of hope.

Of course in us cultured folk perfect love, sentimentality, softness of fibre, heedlessness, forgetfulness, and general superficiality of life — to make a very inadequate list — have combined to cast out fear, "for fear hath torment"; and we thank God loudly that we are so much wiser than our benighted ancestors. Even our New England fathers feared God, though they feared nothing else, but we fear only everything else except God and law. But the unlucky scientific wight living and working in the shadow of adamantine law remains in hopeless bondage to fear.

"Nach ewigen ehernen, grossen Gesetzen
　Mussen wir alle unseres Daseins Kreise vollenden." [1]

These great powers might not necessarily be hopelessly hostile. They might be appeased or won over, possibly controlled. What could he

[1] 292.

do to please them? For something must be done. Here ritual arises.[1] Possibly he offers to one or more of them a share in the feast which he so much enjoys after a successful hunt. In time this may become a sacrifice, sent up and out on the wings of fire.[2] Or he practises a wind or rain dance as the outlet and expression of his intense desire; and to awaken, encourage, and help the powers of these elements. He holds a hunting-dance to rehearse and gain power for the killing of the bear. Call it objectification of his heart's desire, or magic if you prefer. Magic and religion grow up side by side, and probably from the same root in these early stages: as alchemy and chemistry, astrology and astronomy will spring up later.

The pictures on the cave-walls of France probably had a magical or religious purpose. Here we find very few representations of human beings. But in a rock-painting at Cogul, possibly Neolithic though probably older, we see a group of women apparently engaged in some rite of magic or religion. The occurrence of amulets also does not surprise us.

We cannot make a study of primitive ritual magic and religion, their origin, form, and content. But even our hasty glance shows us that

[1] 293.   [2] 294.

man had been wondering and thinking about this subject during millennia before our Neolithic time, had been forced to accept many profound convictions, containing germs of sublime truth overlaid, like our own, with many errors; he had elaborated a system of ritual, and had travelled far along the road of religious experience and discoveries long before this comparatively recent epoch.

The conspicuous features of the religion of this ancient period of primeval stupidity, or *Urdummheit*, to borrow the German word, were the host of invisible powers or dæmons, and the law of taboo, the forbidden thing. Breach of taboo rendered not only the individual lawbreaker but the whole tribe, however innocent, liable to punishment. The whole community was responsible for every deed of any and every one of its members, and suffered or prospered accordingly. When Agamemnon had wronged the priest of Apollo, the god shot his arrows not at Agamemnon but throughout the innocent Greek host. The children of Israel were routed at Ai, because Achan had taken the devoted or forbidden thing. This stage of tribal responsibility seems to be practically universal. It gave the law an iron grip on the people, tamed them, and made them march in lock-step, a necessary stage of terrible discipline. But only under the protection and stimulus of this tribal feeling of common responsibility and resulting tribal conscience could the individual conscience be gradually awakened and developed, and finally break through the cake or crust of custom into freedom and light.

All these forces and influences were acting throughout the Neolithic and later periods, and are still with us. Perhaps we can gain a tolerably distinct and correct view of Neolithic religion among the Mediterranean peoples by a glance at the ancient Greek mysteries. Students of Greek art and literature quite naturally have been very slow to take interest in these crude, often ugly and indecent, rituals. But for this very reason the primitive stands out all the more sharply defined against the brilliant, beautiful, artistic Olympian religion of Greek art and literature, and particularly of Homer. Students like Professor Murray could hardly be expected to explore these lower strata with great sympathy. For this very reason, as somewhat unwilling witnesses to whatever is good or great in primitive Greek ritual, their testimony is all the more valuable, though probably hardly as just as that of Miss Harrison.[1]

[1] 309.

We shall follow mainly Professor Murray's vivid
portrayal.[1] In his *Saturnia Regna* he pictures
the ritual and belief of the ancient Greeks before the arrival of Achæans or Hellenes in any
strict sense of the word. Strictly speaking, it is
a description of the religion of the Bronze Age
during the earlier part of the second millennium
B. C. It has been growing, developing, and
undergoing modifications since Neolithic time,
but in all its essential features it is ancient.

We find here very few traces of the chief
Olympian divinities, which belong to a later age
than the objects of worship or cult of these ancient peoples whom we venture to call Pelasgi.
They worshipped powers or dæmons in indefinite
numbers, but with no individual names: represented, if at all, by emblems or symbols, very
rarely in bodily human form. Of these spirits
of death, disease, madness, and calamity there
were "thousands upon thousands, from whom
man can never escape or hide." So much is
mainly a heritage from Paleolithic times. But
the conception of spirit has grown more clear,
distinct, and elevated, as we saw in our study of
burial rites.

But Neolithic men lived in communities and
devoted themselves largely to tillage of the

[1] 307.

ground and to raising sheep, goats, swine, and cattle. Their life was still precarious. "Their food depended on the crops of one tiny plot of ground. All the while they knew almost nothing of the real causes that made crops succeed or fail. They only felt sure it was a matter of pollution, of unexpiated defilement. It is this state of things that explains the curious cruelty of agricultural works, which like most cruelty had its roots in terror, terror of the breach of taboo — the 'Forbidden Thing.'"

Neolithic man, with his new discoveries and industries, had given new hostages to fortune, and a new and wider scope of application to the old doctrine of taboo and of tribal responsibility. This strengthened the hold of the priest or magician on the hopes, fears, and faith of his people. The law is going deeper as well as wider. There arises an individual feeling of pollution and of the need of expiation which will blaze out in the oldest Greek tragedies as almost a veritable sense of sin. We might almost say that a sense of morality toward the spirit world is now appearing in a religion previously almost or quite unmoral. We may easily overestimate the extent and power of the change, but we can hardly be mistaken in recognizing its dawn and the vast germinal possibilities of this dim feeling or conception.

In agriculture and throughout nature seed-time was followed by harvest, fall, and winter's gloom and death. Then in the next spring there was a return, a rebirth or a resurrection. If the seed failed to come up, if the blade withered or was blighted, it was because the vegetation spirit or dæmon had failed to reappear or had been re-born weak or sickly, and all this because some one had broken taboo, had touched the forbidden thing. This must be prevented at all cost, they must help the spirit. Hence there must be every year a time of purification, of renovation, when the old garments and utensils and everything which could carry the pollution of death were cast off or cleansed.

All these conclusions, and some others of equal importance to which we will return later, are expressed or symbolized in the great Dro-mena, festivals, mysteries, or whatever you may call these rites of pre-Homeric Greece. Then, for a time, they are partially, though never totally, eclipsed, by the brilliant beauty of the Olympian religion with its glorious temples, statues, and other works of art.

The Olympian gods had conquered the world. They practise neither agriculture nor industry, nor any honest work. They fight and feast and drink and play. They are conquering chieftains, royal buccaneers. The Olympian religion had its time and place, and did its work. It swept out many indecent features of the older cults, many superstitions and abuses. It suited the Achæans and their civilization exactly, and we can never forget its "sheer beauty." But it went bankrupt, lost its hold on men's minds and hearts, failed and faded out. Professor Murray compares its end to that of a garden of rare exotic flowers overrun by the rank weeds which it had temporarily displaced. Miss Harrison more justly compares it to a flower withering because cut off from its roots.

There was vastly more vitality in the ancient crude symbols and chaos of conceptions than in the ordered and artistic Olympian hierarchy with its marvellous representations of the gods in human or superhuman form and beauty. Even its art and literature could not save it. It had lost its mysticism. The old Neolithic religion, handed down by peasants and artisans reoccupied the field, transformed sometimes almost beyond recognition, like the Ugly Duckling of the fairy tale. It returned triumphant through sheer power of unlimited vitality and adaptability. Plato draws his finest illustrations from its mysteries, out of which, also, the Greek drama arose. Paul quotes from them or from a similar stratum of belief.

Some of the many sources of its vitality are obvious. It was rooted in the firm conviction of the existence of a spiritual world toward and into which its every rootlet was forcing its way and from which it drew nourishment and power. We might better change the illustration and say that it was slowly developing a spiritual eye which peered into a higher world and developed in keenness and clearness of vision in response to the higher pulsations. By patient experiment and experience, which produced a hope that could not make ashamed and a faith in which hope and experiment combined, it was feeling its way into spiritual knowledge. It knew nothing of practical science or of material cause and effect. But its world pulsated with the universal life. It recognized the law of forbidden things and the sure penalty of lawbreaking. It had a tribal conscience and recognized the need of purification. It had the promise, at least, of individual conscience and consciousness of sin.

Its symbol was the mystery which lifted only a corner of the veil and left an abundant opportunity for wonder, imagination, thought, and mysticism, which was entirely lacking in the perfect statue and the finished creed. It made man, through its sympathetic magic, a coworker with his divinities or dæmons in gaining the answer to an intensive desire or prayer acted by all the members of the community with all their united might, instead of expressed merely in words, the utterance of his whole being and life. Such a system or chaos overflows with sublime possibilities.

The introduction of agriculture had produced another most important change in religious views and ritual. In tillage the earth brought forth and gave birth to the crops which furnished their chief food supply, and probably, in their view, to animals and men also; just as the human mother gives birth to the child. Hence there was a wide-spread belief in, and cult of, an earth divinity, of course female, or in a goddess or dæmon of fertility. She is sometimes or usually accompanied by a male partner, companion or son, but he occupies a lower place.

This cult of the goddess seems to have been a marked feature of Neolithic religion.[1] We find it in the remains of the Minoan periods in Crete; Isis and her companion god Osiris were very prominent in Egypt. The cult was widespread throughout Asia Minor: Diana, or better Artemis, of the Ephesians, Ma in Anatolia, the

[1] 315–319.

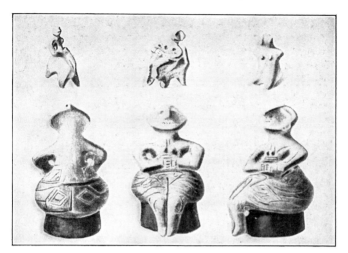

FEMALE IDOLS, THRACE

FEMALE IDOL, ANAU

great goddess of the Hittites are a few examples. Farther eastward we find Astarte. Pumpelly found a female idol (Astarte?) at Anau. The cult dots, if it does not cover, the old middle migration route. We remember the wide-spread distribution of the painted pottery from Susa to Anau and over to Boghaz-keui in the land of the Hittites. Art and religion are closely related during the early times and a wide-spread type of art suggests, though it does not prove, an accompanying form of religion similar throughout the same wide area. In Greece we find Demeter, and in "Pelasgic Athens" the goddess Athena always held the highest place. Hera may well have been another great goddess of the Pelasgi. When the conquering Achæans came in and their chieftains wedded the princesses of the land, they married their god Zeus to the goddess of the land. Hence this cult has been displaced and its records blotted out by later changes. That so many traces of it outlasted the Bronze Age is a proof of its firm hold and great vitality.

We have studied these ancient cults in Greece and the Mediterranean basin because here they are easily discovered and can be restored. They are covered by only a thin layer of later cults which could not destroy their vitality. When we attempt to explore northern Europe the situation is quite different. Christianity blotted out all traces of the worship of Odin and Thor; what it could not blot out it took over into its own service in a modified form. Behind Thor and Odin we see the shadowy form of Dyaus (Ziu?), perhaps a sky-god akin to the Hellenic Zeus, whose name has come down to us in our weekday, Tuesday. Behind all these we must search for traces of the deeply buried and almost obliterated genuine Neolithic cults. These traces could persist only as superstitions of peasants.

We notice first of all that we find one race extending northward along the coast of France into England and Denmark, the zone of the megalithic monuments. In this zone we find figurines and carvings of divinities. Here Déchelette tells us that the female divinity was undoubtedly preferred as the guardian of the tombs.[1] This zone was so closely connected with the Mediterranean region that we should expect nothing else.

In southeastern Europe, around the valley of the Danube, at Cucuteni, Jablanica, and elsewhere, we find figurines, and here again the female divinity is at least the more prominent, if

[1] A: 594–603, 362.

not decidedly dominant.[1] Déchelette tells us as
to its source: "From the earliest times striking
analogies have been proven between the old
villages of the Danube and the Balkans and the
Ægean settlements of the Troad and Phrygia.
Primitive idols, painted pottery, frequent em-
ployment of the spiral in decorative art: all
these occur scattered through the stations of
southeastern Europe in Neolithic times and in
the eastern Mediterranean basin in pre-Mycenæan and Mycenæan days. Between Butmir
(near Sarajevo, Bosnia) and Hissarlik (Troy)
these discoveries mark the routes which without
doubt were already opening communication between the pre-Hellenic peoples and the pre-
Celtic tribes." Reinach adds: "Eastern Europe,
part of Asia Minor and of Egypt, have been re-
vealed as very intense centres of Neolithic civilization."[2] They may be traced in rare examples still farther northward into Bohemia and
even in Thuringia. But their distribution outside of southeastern Europe is very sparse.
Traces of the worship of an earth mother,[3]
though vague and few, can still be discovered
in the superstitions of the peasant folk of northern Germany. A primitive belief in spirits of
the earth, of vegetation, of fertility — of dæmons

[1] B: II, 563.　　　　　[2] 320.　　　　　[3] 316.

who preside over the crops, who die in the autumn or winter and reappear in the spring — is common in the folk-lore and customs of the peasants in many parts of Europe. Our May-pole has an interesting history and is probably the last survival of an ancient cult. Still other more interesting illustrations might easily be cited.[1]

The Balder-myth is familiar to us all. He is a "rare exotic," entirely out of place in that circle of berserker gods and brutal giants who lived in or over against the Norse Valhalla, but would have found himself at home in the land and times of Dionysus. Have we possibly here an intrusion of a far more ancient religious element which even the rude dwellers in a harsh Northland could not forget, and would not allow to die?

Usually accompanying the cult of the goddess we find frequent and wide-spread traces of a related trend of thought, mother-right (Mut-terrecht), maternal kinship, matriarchy: under which were generally included the reckoning of descent in the female line, rights of inheritance by the daughter, hence female rights of property and general high social and economic position of woman. These features need not be united —

[1] 322.

they may appear separately, one here and another there. We are probably not studying a system of thought or law, but a general tendency of life.[1]

Mother-right, to use the most general term, survived, partially at least, down to historic time in Egypt. It persisted in Asia Minor. Perhaps it crops out in the story of the Amazons. We find traces of it in ancient law and custom in northern Europe. Says Hoernes: "Among the Greeks, Romans, Celts, Germans, and Slavs, remains of mother-right occur even in historic times."[2] Wundt thinks that maternal kinship was once universal.[3] We have no time or room to discuss the origin of mother-kinship. We may yet find that it and mother-right represent distinct forms of a deep-seated universal tendency, often of independent origin, occurring usually together but sometimes separate.

Something akin to mother-right, and to a high position and dominating influence of woman in the family and in society, is only what we should expect at this time. We have seen that women were the first great discoverers and inventors; discoverers and founders of all our household arts and crafts as well as of most of our science. Women were the first spinners

[1] 318, 321.   [2] B: II, 585.   [3] O: 173.

and weavers, the first potters. They were the first herbalists and botanists and the first household physicians. In the care of the children they were compelled to be alert, quick-minded, ready for all sorts of emergencies. Paleolithic man was a mere hunter; the rest of the time he ate and loafed. The woman provided the vegetable food, as well as much of the animal, and became the first gardener or farmer. She introduced tillage of the ground, and thus became economically by far the more important member of the partnership, and she probably had by far the more alert, quick-witted brain.

The establishment of agriculture was followed by the cult of the earth-mother, who gave birth to all the fruits of the ground and probably to all life. The goddess, with or without a male companion, was the head of the hierarchy. This again could not have been without its influence. Says Miss Harrison: "Woman to primitive man is a thing at once weak and magical, to be oppressed, yet feared. She is charged with powers of child-bearing denied to man, powers only half understood, sources of attraction but also of danger and repulsion, forces that all over the world seem to fill him with dim terror. The attitude of man to woman and, though perhaps to a less degree, of woman to man is still essentially magical. Man cannot escape being born of woman: but he can, and if he is wise he will, as soon as he comes to manhood, perform ceremonies of riddance and purgation."[1]

One other fact deserves notice. In times of dearth the savage man always eats up all the grain reserved as seed for the next year, and there is none to sow. This is the rock on which attempts to introduce agriculture among savages or nomads have usually been shipwrecked. Here the priest, or perhaps priestess, of the goddess came to her aid, armed with the weapon of taboo. Against this alliance the poor, stupid, clumsy, and slow-witted Neolithic man struggled in vain. He could vent his fury by pulling his wife about by the hair, but this availed little or naught. He had to submit and be resigned.

Female magic increases in power as we approach the frontier and frontier life. At the fall of the Roman Empire northern tribes swept away the old civilization. Grass grew in the ruined cities, only villages remained inhabited. The priests, by a liberal preaching of hell and other dire torments, attempted to subdue these barbarians to law and to introduce order. Agriculture and industry rearose or returned slowly. Finally after the "dark ages" great cathedrals

[1] 308: 36.

sprang up, dedicated not to apostles or martyrs but to the Virgin, Queen of Heaven. Mr. Adams tells us that at this time the women of France were the real leaders. Is this apparent parallelism mere chance, or is it due to a certain amount of similarity in conditions?

Some one has said that our Neolithic ancestors, especially the megalith-builders, were priest-ridden. If he had added that they were tamed and led, and very possibly diligently hen-pecked, by a veritable matriarchate, I suspect that he would have discovered and correctly estimated the two great sources of their marvellous progress. For at this stage, as at some others, the priests and the women were the élite, and the government was, therefore, ideal for its day.

But the tendency was based upon something far broader and deeper than changing social and economic conditions and religious feeling. Even the "mere man" must admit that it was biological and natural. "Nature," says Humboldt, "has taken woman under her special protection." She has always been partial to the female. Throughout the long period of mammalian evolution she has showed very little regard for the males. The more they fight and kill one another off, the fewer useless individuals to feed. The same tendency reaches its logical conclusion in the parthenogenesis of insects. Havelock Ellis says of woman: "She bears the special characteristics of humanity in a higher degree than man, and represents more nearly than man the human type which man is approximating." He boldly asserts that man seems to be the "weaker vessel," and brings strong arguments for his assertion.[1]

> "Das Ewig-weibliche
> Zieht uns hinan."

The buried Pelasgic religion regained its rightful place. It had more vital reality than the Olympian. Has the great Roman Catholic Church, in its worship of the Virgin, retained at least the symbol of an element of vital reality which we Protestants, in our recoil from so-called "Mariolatry," have neglected to our cost in favor of a purely paternal conception of God? We leave this question to the theologians.

[1] 330.

CHAPTER XI

PROGRESS

IT is a far cry and long and weary road from the ape descending from the trees and the ape-man shuffling over the ground, keeping close to his arboreal refuge, to the lake-dweller and builder of stone monuments. There was very little in the appearance or structure of the ape-man to encourage great hopes for the future. The sleek, graceful, wiry, well-armed cats were far more attractive, promising, and thrilling actors on the world's stage. Why did not they progress, win the future, and insure that all the future meetings of art and learning should be held on the back fence? They certainly did not progress — that is a stubborn fact.

They had largely or completely exhausted the possibilities of their special line of development; as cats they were perfect and could dominate the portion of the world in which as cats they were solely interested. This was an impassable bar to progress. Why should they change? They were so thoroughly conformed to the environment of their time and conditions that any marked change would have been a disadvantage. But when conditions did change, and the fashion of the world which had produced them passed away, they became out of fashion, "back numbers," incapable of meeting new emergencies and crises — like men, parties, and governments in all ages of human history. They suffered from overadaptation and the resulting limitations.

Man did not make this mistake. Isolated tribes and even races might settle down in contentment, become completely adapted to easy conditions of life, and stagnate or degenerate. But a saving remnant was always marching out into new physical or social surroundings, exposed to new needs, fears, and opportunities, and readapting itself to meet and profit by them. Man was not, and could not be, precocious. He was always a bundle of possibilities and great expectations, which he has even now only begun to realize.

Overpopulation, or other pressure in his primeval home, resulted in great racial migrations, sending him all over the world to seek his fortune. He became one of the very few physically cosmopolitan animals, living everywhere from the equator to the Arctic zone. He became toughened and hardened and adaptable, able to live under the most trying circumstances. Everywhere he had to be a close observer, watchful and wary. He was weak and defenseless, and his life depended upon his quick recognition of "nature's signs of displeasure," upon the full exercise of his few small wits. He learned to be faithful in a few things. We need not repeat or review this weary chapter of his history.

"There were years that no one talked of. There were times of horrid doubt.
There was faith and hope and whacking and despair."

Man was experimenting with all kinds of climates and conditions. It was in the hard and cold northern regions that he developed farthest, though less rapidly at first. We have already glanced at the educational results of language, of family life in the rock-shelter around the fire, of the fashioning and use of tools, of his love of ornaments and display, of his dawning and clearing self-consciousness, of the beginnings of ownership. We have noticed his burial rites and their suggestions. All these may have been rude and crude, but they contained the germs of vast possibilities, though painfully slow of development. His "castles in Spain" were his richest possessions, though he probably never knew or suspected them. One hundred thousand years of human life in Europe produced nothing higher than Neanderthal man.

Suddenly, at the beginning of Upper Pale-olithic time Cro-Magnon man appeared. His splendid physique and large brain, his produc-tion and appreciation of art, and many other qualities, have led some one to speak of him as the "prehistoric Greek." In our enthusiasm we may easily overestimate his powers; but, as we study him and his work, we feel that here was a great race, and that now some great human possibilities are to be fully attained and made permanent. Apparently he had come from the plateau region of western Asia. Near his birth-place there must have been other peoples ca-pable of great things. We remember that Susa was probably founded not much later than the beginning of the Magdalenian epoch in Europe. But the Cro-Magnon folk decreased in numbers, in stature, apparently also in ability and vitality. During the period of transition to Neolithic time Europe was occupied only by a sparse population of fishermen along the rivers, while barbarous hunting tribes were working their way north-ward toward the Baltic. The shell-heaps of Denmark are the monuments of the attainments of this epoch.

A higher civilization had already entered the Mediterranean basin. It was building houses, villages, possibly forerunners of the Greek city-

states. Especially in Greece they were sufficiently separated to allow independence of development and great variety, and yet near
enough to one another to prevent the ill effects
of complete isolation. Here there was rapid
interchange and improvement of physical and
mental attainments, mental stimulation and
rivalry, change and progress. Implements,
weapons, pottery; new discoveries, inventions,
ideas, arts, and habits of life and thought spread
slowly and gradually from these centres of progressing culture far to the northward. This was
undoubtedly one important source of stimuli.
But we must not overestimate its influence.[1]

It spread through France into England and
Denmark. As time went on this northward
current increased and strengthened until, during
the Bronze period, the Baltic region, especially
Denmark, became almost a second Mediterranean centre of culture and art; just as at a
far later time Flemish cities became the Venices
of the north. But the north was never a beg-
garly dependent and imitator of the south. It
selected and accepted only what it would, almost
always modified and frequently improved what
it had selected.

The larger part of central and northern

[1] H: 20.

ANCIENT FISHERMEN

From the mural painting by Fernand Cormon in the Muséum d'Histoire Naturelle, Paris.

Europe lay outside of this great current and was
reached by it only slightly and very indirectly.
These regions or provinces were largely working
out their own civilization and culture.

What then was the real source of Neolithic
progress?[1] It is not to be sought in great wars
and revolutions. Genuine wars are carried on
by nations with a national government, and as
yet there were no nations, and even tribal government — outside of religion, the great bond of
tribal unity at this stage — was probably weak,
loose, and inefficient. There were no such
strong towns or city-states as sprang up later
in Greece. There were here no nomadic hordes
to be driven by drought from their withering
pastures to migrate *en masse* and force their
way into less thirsty and starving regions.
There was, as yet, no great overpopulation of
mountainous areas compelling raids or forays
into piedmont zones. The nearest approach to
this condition is the slow, evidently peaceful
penetration of parts of France by broad-heads
from its eastern uplands filtering in and mixing
with the long-headed older population, and be-
traying their arrival mainly by a change in form
of head and rise of cephalic index.

There was little wealth to tempt invasion.

[1] 179: 122 *n.*

There were no cities or large towns to plunder. There were wide stretches of land thinly or not at all populated and open to any newcomer. All that we know of Neolithic religion, far more dominant in tribal life and action than the very feebly developed political or social organization, the cult of the goddess, and the accompanying mother-right, suggest peace. The great invasions of the Bronze and Iron periods introduced or stimulated the cult of war gods and patriarchal family life and kinship. But these were still in the future. The picture of Europe at this time as a great arena of roving savages, thirsting for blood and always at war, seems to be a caricature.

The people of the banded pottery were evidently peaceful. They left no weapons except mattocks and hammers. No one, I believe, has ever accused the broad-heads of bloodthirst. The graves of northern hunters with corded pottery are all about Grosgartach. The little village was deserted and decayed. It showed no signs of having been burned. The lake-dwellings were open to attack at all times, especially after the ice had formed during the winter. Robenhausen during its long history burned several times; hardly as often as most of our New England villages. Here a single brand or fire-tipped arrow in a thatched roof would have destroyed the whole settlement.

Only in northern Europe, in the country of the corded pottery, do we find great attention paid to the making of fine weapons like the flint daggers and axes. Here we have chiefly herdsmen and hunters. Here there were probably village incompatibilities — Donnybrook fairs, cattle-lifting, and forays. But these should hardly be dignified with the name of wars. We find then some North German peoples at the very end of the Neolithic period pushing southward, often by peaceable infiltration, sometimes perhaps by violent incursions, when the resistance was great.[1]

Says Wundt:[2] "So long as he is not obliged to protect himself against peoples that crowd in upon him, primitive man is familiar with the weapon only as an implement of the chase. The old picture of a war of all with all, as Thomas Hobbes once sketched the natural state of man, is the very reverse of what obtained. The natural condition is one of peace, unless this is disturbed by external circumstances, one of the most important of which is contact with a higher culture."

We remember, also, the fewness of fortified

[1] 260.   [2] O: 111, 33.

villages in northern Europe until toward the end
of the Neolithic period, and then mainly along
great routes of migration; and around mines and
workshops. They seem to fail altogether in
Scandinavia at this time. Even the wars, battles, or quarrels which occurred probably hindered progress far more than they aided it.
Haeckel in his younger days was fierce in his
denunciations of the stupidity of war.

Political or economic revolutions could hardly
occur when there was probably little organized
government and even less wealth and class
difference.

Conditions in France may have been somewhat different. Here the great stone monuments suggest a denser population under a more
advanced organization, religious or political, or
both, reminding us of conditions in the Mediterranean region, with whose culture it was closely
connected. Here fortifications seem to have
been quite numerous.[1] But our knowledge is
too slight to allow even a conjecture.

In the southeastern part of Europe we find
the people of the banded pottery who practised
an advanced form of agriculture. Here apparently the men as well as the women worked
in the fields. We find their stone mattocks and

[1] A: 368.

EARLY AGRICULTURE

From the mural painting by Fernand Cormon in the Muséum d'Histoire Naturelle, Paris.

ploughshares. Hoe-culture was giving place to ploughing. Here men were receiving a very different education and training from the hunters, fishermen, and herdsmen of the north, though there also a gradual increase of tillage was doubtless taking place. They were tilling the ground laboriously, monotonously, doing what was wearisome and disagreeable for a reward sometimes large, sometimes scanty. The peasant farmer learns forethought, thrift, economy, industry, and a host of homely virtues, far less known to hunter or herdsman. He is no more a collector taking what he finds: he has gone into partnership with nature. He is studying her ways, moods, and whims. He amasses a steadily increasing store of most valuable lore concerning climate, weather, soil, plants, animals, and things. He is rooted in a little patch of ground. His outlook is narrow and he is slow to change. But he learns his lessons thoroughly. He may enter the school unwillingly but he stays in it.

He has a permanent home even if it is hardly more than a hut, which is the centre of his life and thought. It is a hard, healthy life, and population increases rapidly under such conditions. He probably has a large family of children, and they educate and socialize him and one another. He is trained and moulded by "home surroundings." Is not this the history of the frontiersman or homesteader everywhere at all times? The home and family attachments and instincts are deeply rooted because very ancient and entirely natural.

He lives in a village or neighborhood, which is hardly more than a great patriarchal family, closely united by intermarriage, and by the pressure of common work to satisfy common needs, common ownership of the soil, mutual aid in hard times. The religious rites and ceremonies, the feasts and mysteries, the prayers or magic, are all community affairs. Many of the divinities are local. These religious bonds are all the firmer and more compelling because, in the lack of any developed and permanent political organization, religion is the great tribal bond. We easily forget the civilizing, refining, and improving unremitting pressure and power of these simple, uninteresting peasant influences. He is learning to get on with the members of the family and neighborhood. He is experimenting upon his neighbors: his experiments and experiences may often be very trying to himself and them; the results may sometimes be discouraging. But he is not only practising the essentials and fundamentals of morality, very incomplete and without code; but a sort of preparatory course in government. It may easily be self-government in these small villages. The town-meeting originated here or somewhat farther north.

We have already seen that his religion had grown out of the experiences of his daily life. May we not claim that science and a sort of philosophy may have sprung from the same source? He knew nothing of cause and effect in the material world. But he was seeking diligently the invisible bond of relations of things and events. The relation, according to his views, was mainly of a spiritual character through the agency of dæmons. His ritual, call it magic if you will, was the expression of his conviction that results in the material world might be modified by his lending a helping hand to all the beneficent spirits. He indulged freely in hypotheses, but these were the outgrowth of millennia of experience and life, a very healthy form of pragmatism. He who has never laughed at a modern scientific theory, useful and fruitful in its time but now outgrown and replaced by a somewhat better one, may cast the first stone at his "benighted" Neolithic ancestor.

We might even venture to suspect that in his own crude way he was a philosopher. He must have had something like a philosophy of life, even if it was hardly more than a dumb instinct.

Says Miss Harrison: "Dike" (usually translated justice), "in common Greek parlance is the way of life, normal habit. Dike is the way of the world, the way things happen, and Themis is that specialized way for human beings which is sanctioned by the collective conscience, by herd instinct. A lonely beast in the valley, a fish in the sea, has his Dike, but it is not till man congregates together that he has his Themis. Greeks and Indians alike seem to have discovered that the divine way was also the truth and the life. This notion of the way, which was also the truth and the life, seems to have existed before the separation of Indian from Iranian. Closely allied to Dike and to Vedic Rta is the Chinese Tao, only it seems less moralized and more magical. Deep-rooted in man's heart is the pathetic conviction that moral goodness and material prosperity go together, that if man keep the Rta, he can magically affect for good nature's ordered going." [1]

Thus primitive man, long before the dawn of anything like civilization, was seeking, finding, clearing, and treading out the "way" to an ordered, right, and healthy individual and social

[1] 308.

life — not through, but to, codes of morals and systems of philosophy. His thought was more or less chaotic, perhaps; it was crudely, often indecently, expressed in ugly form or action; but it was always acted upon, kept close to life. We might possibly call him an "Ur-pragmatist," if you will pardon the barbarism. He had neither the language nor the "conveniences for thinking" and other things, to write out a cool, logical abstract system in long words. In this we have outrun him until we have left him out of sight. His philosophy was not a guide-book or map, but a rough and often miry trail.

We have tried to express briefly the results of a glance at the agriculturists of southeastern Europe. Before the close of the Neolithic period they were in fairly close communication with Ægean culture and owed considerable or much progress to stimuli from this source. In the great essentials of human training and development something quite similar might be said of the lake-dwellers and the broad-heads of eastern France. North Germany had a different culture and probably somewhat different religious cults and general views and conceptions. France and England, too, represented a quite distinct province whose peoples were always under Mediterranean influence. Denmark was already a meeting-place for a variety of cultures, thoughts, and influences.

Peoples were gradually closing in from all directions on the central provinces of northern Europe, and here apparently they met. We find here a mixture of head-forms, of culture; mixture or modifications of styles of ceramic ornament, of burial customs — all suggesting a mingling of peoples of a variety of cultures. Here at or toward the end of the Neolithic period was the "melting-pot" for the fusion of these peoples and their cultures. There was conflict of customs and ideas, of *ways* of life. There was probably much incompatibility, many broken heads. The pacific people of the banded pottery seem largely to have withdrawn, or been driven out, before the infiltration or invasions of northern folk. It was hardly a comfortable place for conservative pacificists. There were doubtless battles in many regions — perhaps now and here we might speak of wars. In some places there may have been extermination of the fighting men. But in most parts there was large fusion, and out of this mixture of cultures, ideas, thoughts, and habits of life came the culture of the beginning of the Bronze Age.

The great characteristic of Neolithic culture seems to be a rude, often barbarous, sometimes

ugly but generally healthy, always hardy and
vigorous growth — it grew "like a weed" — the
manifestation of an intense vitality. Because
it was healthy it was essentially and generally
fairly sane, matter-of-fact, whole, and balanced.
The Neoliths were certainly no "reversed crip-
ples," in whom one or two of the less essential
powers had outgrown and dwarfed the man. It
was an adaptable stock giving rise to many
marked and vigorous varieties, from whose intercrossing something great and good could
hardly fail to arise.

Green refuses to write a "trumpet-and-drum
history of England." "Happy the people —
here we cannot say nation — that has no an-
nals." Here is surely a certain amount of
truth which we may be in danger of forgetting.
In plants, and often in men, a long period of
silent unnoticeable growth usually precedes the
brief season of flowers and fruit. Is this the
rule in racial, or internal, development?

Is it true, as some historians tell us, that a
dormant period of national history best repays
investigation, and that dormant peoples will
bear watching? Is the dormant nation often
storing up nutriment, strength, vitality, just as
the plant is doing in its ugly underground roots
and stem? Are fallow periods necessary to its

fertility and apparently dormant times essential to its life and growth? Must periods of energetic action and effort be followed by times of exhaustion and rest, as in the history of the strong athlete rejoicing to run a race?

Is China awakening from just such a dormant period? What of India, still the home of philosophy? Because a nation, after bearing a marvellous harvest of culture, thought, art, or religion, seems barren and exhausted, does this discourage or arouse the hope that it will some day produce an equal or greater fruitage?

How about "darkest Africa"? Here surely we have a case of degeneration beyond all hope of recovery, not to mention a great future. But is this quite as certain as some of us seem to think? Is not much of our so-called Occidental progress really an orgy of wasted energy, neurotic excitement, half-camouflaged decadence, which will end in degeneration? We do not know yet. May there some day be a family rather than league of nations to which every one will contribute according to its special ability? If this be granted, will Huxley's statement concerning the individual be applicable to races and peoples: "Its aim will be not so much the survival of the fittest as the fitting of as many as possible to survive"? These are sphinx questions demanding an answer from statesmen. Unfortunately most of our statesmen are only waiting to be gathered to their fathers in the graveyard of dead politicians. We will turn homeward after our excursion, gladly leaving our little bundle of facts and questions at the door of the philosopher of history.

But one question confronts us directly. Is our whole estimate and valuation of Neolithic life, work, and progress extreme and practically worthless? Were they, in spite of all our arguments, a mob of crude, worthless barbarians, undeserving of any gratitude or sympathy, much less of respect? Do we really owe anything to them?

One historic event of great importance had its growth and rise during the Neolithic period out of Neolithic life, conditions, and culture. This was the Aryan culture of Persia and India, of Greece and Rome, and of our northern ancestors. No one seems to deny its importance and value. We must glance at its origin and growth, and see if it supports at all the tentative and often conjectural conclusions at which we have arrived. This will be the object of our work and study in the next and closing chapter.

CHAPTER XII

THE COMING OF THE INDO-EUROPEANS

SAID Max Müller in his *Biographies of Words* : "I have declared again and again that, if I say Aryan, I mean neither blood nor bones, nor hair nor skull; I mean simply those who speak an Aryan language. The same applies to Hindus, Greeks, Romans, Germans, Celts, and Slavs. When I speak of them I commit myself to no anatomical characteristics. The blue-eyed and fair-haired Scandinavians may have been conquerors or conquered, they may have adopted the language of their darker lords or their subjects, or vice versa. I assert nothing beyond their language. . . . To me an ethnologist who speaks of Aryan race, Aryan blood, Aryan eyes and hair, is as great a sinner as a linguist who speaks of a dolichocephalic dictionary or a brachycephalic grammar."

We may well take this warning to heart, and remember that the first and most noticeable, if not the one essential, characteristic of the Aryans was their language. For the sake of convenience and clearness, and of avoiding misunderstanding or prejudice, we will use the word Indo-European for the whole group of languages to which Müller applied the word Aryan. These languages fall into two great divisions or branches: (1) the Indian and Iranian (Persian), which we will call Aryan; and (2) the European branch, including Greek, Latin, German, Slavic, and others. Our first question is: what inferences can we safely draw from a study and comparison of these different European and Asiatic languages? Evidently they have all sprung from a parent language no longer adequately represented by any one of them. They have all been considerably or greatly modified during the lapse of time. They, and others whose names we have omitted, are all sister languages descended or developed from a parent language which must once have been spoken by a people, very probably representing a mixture of races, having a definite local habitation, cradle, or home. Here the language originated as the expression of a certain culture or civilization, and from this region, large or small, it spread into Persia and India and throughout Europe. The wide spread of the language testifies to the superiority in some important respects of either language, culture, people, or all three. We may well recognize two homes, the first, original cradle of the language and culture, and the second homeland, far more extensive, over which the original language, probably with well-marked dialects, was used just before the final separation and dispersal.

In its distribution from India to western Europe it must often have wandered far from its original home. Its introducers must often have been few compared with the large and dense populations among which they came. The Aryans could have been hardly more than a handful among the peoples of India. Something similar may be said of its introduction into Europe about the close of the Neolithic period. Middle Europe was at this time fairly well populated, at least in its more fertile regions. The bearers of the new language must have represented a ruling, conquering, or otherwise very influential class, else it would never have been accepted by the mass of the people.

When the original or modified Indo-European language, perhaps in several distinct dialects, was introduced into Europe, it was carried to peoples of several or many stocks and languages. These had to learn and acquire it as we acquire a foreign language, but only as a spoken, unwritten language. Probably no one of them acquired it exactly in its original form. It was

almost impossible for them to pronounce all its
consonants or combinations, its "shibboleths."
They retained much of the stress and accent
and more of the cadence of their own tongue.
Similarly at a far later date Latin developed
into the various Romance Languages of modern
Europe.

Under the new conditions content and mean-
ings changed as well as forms of language.
Words little used in the new home, especially
names of objects, might easily be lost, while
others would be replaced by favorite apt words
from the aboriginal language. A name might
be applied to a new object and thus change its
meaning. To cite a familiar modern instance,
the robin redbreast of America is quite a different bird from that of England. For a long
time it was supposed that the occurrence of the
root of the word "beech" in the European languages proved beyond doubt that the language
must have originated in a region where the
beech-tree was common. But the Greek word
derived from the same root means oak; a similar, perhaps not the same, root word in Kurdish
means elm. Our knowledge of the original
meaning of the word is very uncertain. Through
all the languages there runs a single word for
weaving or plaiting, but whether the original

word referred to the weaving of cloth or to the plaiting of mats or baskets we do not know.

The work of discovering and restoring the original language is difficult and far from finished. But the comparative philologists or "linguistic paleontologists" have established certain facts, or at least theories, on which we may rely with a fair degree of confidence. We find names for all the most important domestic animals, including the horse. There are words for the wagon, its wheels, and various other parts. Words for tillage and land cultivation agree in the Western branch, but are far less noticeable in the Aryan languages. Here the vocabulary is rather that of the herdsman. This seems to allow us to conclude that, when Eastern and Western branches separated, and probably long before that time, the Eastern people were herdsmen paying slight attention to agriculture: the Western predominantly tillers of the ground.

The linguist, as we have already seen, is frequently or usually unable to discover the exact meaning of the word in the original language, and hence is uncertain as to the degree of development of any art or technique. But the culture, as far as discovered, seems to be that of the average of Neolithic peoples, perhaps fairly well represented by that of the Swiss lake-dwellers. It may have varied in different areas or provinces. The language seems to represent most clearly features of the undivided life and settlement of the people or peoples when it had spread over a wide territory and become the property of a large population, otherwise it would be impossible to explain the successive great waves of Indo-European migration. The cradle where the language originated and took form must have been far more limited and the culture simpler.

The original language contains words for summer and winter, ice and snow; it tells of a fairly cold climate. They had a common word for metal, probably copper, hence they were living together after the introduction of this metal. They lived in villages apparently surrounded by a hedge or wall, or some sort of fortification.

The family was decidedly patriarchal. Of the older mother-right scarcely more than traces remain, survivals from an older alien culture. The goddess is no longer supreme. A new divinity, a sky-god, or sun-god, or manifestation of light or brightness had already appeared — the Greek Zeus, Latin Ju-piter, with the same root appearing in all the languages. The earth-goddess is not banished, but remains as consort of the male divinity. The supreme divinity of the religious cult is no longer local. There is in it an element or germ of universality overleaping all provincial boundaries, in many respects a vast improvement over the old Neolithic religions. It generally held its own, but only by adopting much from the older native religions on which it was superimposed, as was the case in Greece.

Indo-Europeanism must have had something to recommend it and make it highly attractive to enable it to spread so fast and far. The language itself, while apparently somewhat clumsy, was certainly rich in conceptions and shades of expression. The clearness and beauty of the religious cult may have attracted some, though this seems doubtful. All these features are inadequate to explain the rapidity and extent of its spread. We must leave this problem for the present.

Even the original language frequently describes the same object or even action by words having very different roots. It shows great variety in synonyms and inflections. Feist compares it with English and considers it a "mixed language" almost from the start, and many facts seem to favor this view. This does not surprise us when we remember that its growth and development were late, during the latter half of Neolithic time, when great movements and minglings of people were taking place and long routes of trade and communication had opened.

The date of the earliest migrations of Indo-European peoples is roughly indicated by the presence of a word for metal, probably copper, in the original undivided language. Aryan names appear in western Asia about 1400 or 1500 B. C. Meyer says that the Achæans had arrived in the southern Balkans as early as 2000 B. C. and reached Greece about 1200 or 1300 B. C.; the Dorians followed about 1100 B. C. We can hardly be far from the truth if we consider that they were in their original home until about 2000 B. C., and that the separation began very soon after. Their development was a product of the Neolithic period, their spread was the striking event of earliest historic times.

Inasmuch as their migrations are so recent, especially when compared with those of the Semites, it ought to be possible for us to discover certain traits which they brought with them from the homeland. The Achæans had apparently marched southward from Hungary or thereabouts through the Balkans into Greece, arriving there not far from 1200 B. C. They did not come in one invading horde but in successive waves, each crowding the other before it. Behind the Achæans came the Dorians, behind them were the Thracians and other wayfarers. Their unit of organization was the band, brotherhood, or clan, each with its own leader, reminding us of the Scotch clans of a century or two ago. They came with their horses and carts, perhaps with war-chariots. They were the "horse-taming" Achæans. They were youthful, red-blooded, irresponsible and irresistible, careless, untamed barbarians, swaggering in from hard battles and long campaigns, having seen the manners and tested the might of many peoples. They came in contact with ancient, settled, staid, conservative Pelasgic wealth and culture. They were the rough riders of their day. They were hard drinkers and fighters; loud, boastful talkers, good-natured if not opposed; good "mixers."

Their chieftains married the princesses of the old régime, who seem to have held the right of succession in the kingdom or city-state. The wooing was rough and more or less forceful; but I suspect that the princesses yielded not altogether unwillingly, even if the course of true love did not always continue to run smooth in after years. They married their gods to the

goddesses of the land, and made little further in-
terference with the old Ægean religion or popular
life.

In comparison with the native peoples who
had builded Tiryns and Mycenæ the Achæans
were probably few, scattered over Greece.
They probably robbed the subject peoples with
one hand, but with the other they defended
them against the forays of sea-pirates and other
enemies.   They were no worse than former native rulers, far better watch-dogs of the city, attractive leaders of an admiring crowd, the best
possible missionaries of a new culture and language.   They turned the old Neolithic world
upside down.   Evolution had brought revolution: old things passed away and, for a time,
all things became new.   We cannot easily overestimate the extent and importance of the
change.

The leaders, and naturally their followers to
a less degree, show clearly the characteristics of
the new era, which Wundt has called the Age of
Heroes in distinction from the Age of Totemism
and the iron supremacy of tribal custom.   The
chief feature was the rise, development, and
dominance of individual personality in the leaders and the enthusiastic, individual loyalty of the
members of the brotherhood or clan.   Up to

this time the individual has been entirely submerged in the customs and culture of the tribe,
whose control has been mostly in the hands of
the old men and the priests; now the young war-
rior and champion has grasped the reins. In
all Homer's pictures the ranks of the common
people, however firm, count for little. The
battle is won in single, hand-to-hand combat by
the leader — a dour giant of an Ajax, a dashing
Menelaus, "good at the rescue," a crafty Ulysses,
a heroic Hector. The wisdom of old Nestor is
endured with kindly tolerance, hardly with enthusiasm. It is an age of young men with all
their virtues and vices. But every leader is
a distinctly marked individual; no two are
alike.

City-states are beginning to appear, but their
success depends very largely on the wisdom and
power of the ruler, who seems at first to be largely
irresponsible, a despot in the ancient sense of
the word. It is anything but a true democracy,
but it is government by the élite of their day
and world. The new era or *Zeitgeist* is putting
its stamp on all its peoples. Homer's description of the Achæans would apply almost equally
well to the Celts when they first appear in history; and kindred spirits are marching and fighting in India and Persia. All seem to represent

a new type which all brought from the common homeland.

The chieftains, with this clan or brotherhood of warlike followers, came into a country occupied by agriculturists or peasants unused and untrained to war, such as we have found in the Mediterranean region and in most of northern Europe. Conquest was usually easy and left little bitterness. There was no national consciousness or pride to arouse resistance. It was a totally different kind of invasion from that of nomadic Semites in Asia, or of Mongols into Europe. It came almost as a new movement, a renaissance for which the people were ready. Celt and Greek alike were usually absorbed and lost in the masses of the people to whom they came. Physically they produced little permanent change in the people with whom they mingled. They seem to have accepted fully as much as they contributed, and may often have received credit for many improvements which they really had little share in bringing about.

We have already seen that Greek philosophy and religion, while retaining much of the Olympian or Indo-European form, sprang essentially from the old Pelasgic cults with their greater vitality. How far were Achæans and Dorians responsible for the glory of Greek art, especially in "Pelasgic Athens"? The answer can hardly be as obvious and sure as it has appeared to some.

How far was Roman government and law due to Indo-European influence? Neither Greeks nor Celts seem to have been very successful in founding great or permanent states. Italy was far less easy of access from the north than from Greece, and Rome lay well southward beyond the Apennines. Some of its most important political features seem to have sprung from uprisings of the *Plebs*, the common people, probably mostly of native stock; others, perhaps, from the Etruscans. I cannot attempt to answer this question or any one of many similar ones. The Indo-Europeans brought in a new era and started a new world; but just what was their definite and permanent contribution to European culture?

Europe had been long enough in the school of Neolithic discipline. Agriculture and settled home life had trained peasants to do many things which they disliked to do, to observe taboo and to obey ancient custom, to march in rank and file, and even in lock-step. It was a hard school in which savage man had been tamed, home-broken, and socialized, and he had learned its lessons thoroughly. It was high time that men should be promoted to a higher grade of education the aim of whose training should be the development of free and vigorous personality. The crust or cake of custom must yield or be broken and allow the individual to enter upon the possession of his rights.

It was a critical and revolutionary change. It had been rendered easier by the accumulation of wealth, and of a certain amount of personal property in cattle and other goods. In centres of trade the individual was thrown more and more on his own resources and initiative. With exchange of goods came exchange of knowledge, ideas, and methods undermining the ancient customs and traditions. Movements or migrations of peoples or smaller bands called for leadership by the most capable. And those became more and more numerous about the close of the Neolithic period. Neolithic culture had been largely the product of peace and isolation; it was inadequate to the new conditions. Matriarchy and the cult of the goddess were unsuited to times of struggle and migration; with the rise of the chieftain comes the worship of the war-god.

Where did this change or revolution and the rise of this new language and culture and remarkable people take place? All agree that the cradle or original homeland must have been

somewhere on our third route of migration, the
great zone of steppe and parkland stretching
from western Turkestan westward along the
Caspian and Black Seas into the valley of the
Danube, and from the Hungarian extension of
the Asiatic steppe northward to the great plain
of North Germany and to Scandinavia. In our
study of racial migrations we found that the
great Mongoloid branch went eastward from the
neighborhood of the Iranian plateau, while successive waves of migration turned westward into
Europe, both following a zone of steppe and
parkland enjoying unusually favorable climatic
conditions in early Postglacial times.

The discovery of Sanskrit and the belief that
it represented the parent of the Indo-European
languages led students to place the original
centre of their dispersal far toward the eastern
end of this zone. When it became evident that
this view of Sanskrit was untenable, they began
to locate the centre in Europe. Finally some
or many students have sought it in the extreme
west and north in Germany or also in Scandinavia. When careful and thorough scholars
have arrived at so many and so different conclusions, we may well be cautious and remember
that new discoveries may necessitate a change
in our own views.

The chief argument in favor of the North German homeland is anthropological. The earliest Indo-Europeans both in Europe and Asia were apparently blonds, with light hair and eyes; and such people have lived along the shore of the Baltic since early Neolithic times.

The claim that the ancient Celts and Achæans were physically more like Germans and Scandinavians than any other European people is certainly not without foundation. It has been urged that the Indo-Europeans were acquainted with the sea and with the eel, which is said to be unknown in the tributaries of the Black and Caspian Seas, as also their acquaintance with the beech. Other arguments can be found in special articles. We have seen that arguments based on the meaning of words like beech, eel, and sea, rest on a very insecure foundation. The Finns are almost as blond as the Germans, and Kossina[1] places them with the Germans as

[1] I have selected for examination Professor Kossina's article, and that not his latest, because it seems to furnish the strongest and clearest brief statement of the theory of the Germanic origin of the Indo-Europeans. Hirt's work and his references should also be consulted. It is to be regretted that the judgment and work of some of the North German prehistorians on this question are tinged by national prejudice. We must make allowance for their omissions and remember that we have our own pet prejudices.

The dogma of the superiority of the dolichocephalic blond has been made a cult by Mr. J. H. Chamberlin and other far less brilliant writers. It has received little support in Scandinavia. The works of this school should not be taken too seriously.

ancestors of the Indo-Europeans. There are in Europe also blond brachycephals, generally acknowledged to have been of western Asiatic origin. The arguments for a Germanic origin are attractive, but hardly convincing, and anything but conclusive.

The objections to this view are weighty. One marked feature of Indo-European culture was the use of the horse, which held the highest rank among their domestic animals. But the domestic horse seems to have been introduced into Europe from the East. The few traces of its presence in northern Europe during Neolithic times are usually explained as remains of wild animals killed in the hunt. If they played so large a part in Indo-European culture, it is strange that they have left so few remains.

Kossina, in one of his studies, places the cradle of Indo-European culture in "Scandinavia, Denmark, and northwest Germany, wherever megalithic monuments with their characteristic pottery occur." Wherever such monuments occur we find incineration coming in late in Neolithic time, or more exactly with the Bronze period, except in Brittany and England, of which later. But incineration seems to accompany the progress of the European branch, and must have come into use among these peoples well back in their history to explain its wide occurrence.

The word town, in the original language, seems to signify a settlement surrounded by a hedge or wall, or some sort of defense. But fortified towns are hardly known in North Germany at this time. All these cultural features seem to appear somewhat or considerably too late in North Germany to suit Kossina's theory.

A second feature of Indo-European culture is the rise of the chieftain. But the Germans seem to have borrowed the name for king and other expressions for military organizations, as well as many culture-words, from the Celts. This fact has led some good authorities to declare that the Germans received their Indo-European language from the Celts.

The homeland of the Indo-Europeans must have supported a large population to send out all the tribes which went out from it. Only such a region can satisfy our requirements, and such was Germany, an *Officina gentium*, some 2,000 years later. But we notice that the migrations of peoples have always set westward into Europe, not in the reverse direction. Similarly the new discovery or idea has come westward or northward from western Asia or from the Mediterranean region. The north has almost never been a centre of origination of new ideas and movements. It has borrowed from the richer south. We would not expect that the

Indo-European movement would form an exception to this rule. Moreover, the peoples of the banded pottery who had filled southeastern Europe, coming in, as is generally acknowledged, from the East, had brought with them a good knowledge of agriculture which could support a large population.

Now Kossina finds evidence of the spread of the corded pottery southward at the close of the Neolithic period, and infers that it was carried by a migration from the north. I am inclined to think that his conclusion is correct, though it may be doubtful whether the invasion went so far into the province of the banded pottery as he thinks. He sees in this the first stage of the Indo-European movement which was to sweep eastward as far as India. The people of the banded pottery apparently retreated eastward before this movement, and thus tended still further to increase the density and power of resistance in these regions. Furthermore, had this southeastward movement continued, it would have met the first of a series of waves of invasion which would surely have turned it backward.

We have seen that all through the Neolithic period brachycephals of the Furfooz or Grenelle race have been spreading from Belgium and the

rough eastern part of France. At the end of
the Neolithic period they are being crowded by
the long-heads. During the Bronze Age the
cephalic index rises all over middle and western
Europe. At its very beginning we find a new
people in England — tall, rugged, heavy-faced
round-heads, who burned their dead and deposited the ashes in round barrows. They seem
to have come from the Rhine valley, and may
well have introduced incineration into Brittany,
where it appears early. They differ markedly
in stature and features from the Furfooz people.
They have quite certainly come from the east,
perhaps from the region of the Armenian highlands. They have crossed Europe in sufficient
numbers and compactness to retain their anthropological characters until they strike England and crowd back the old Iberian or Mediterranean peoples. The movement looks like an
invasion in mass, not like a quiet, slow infiltration. They were the forerunners of a general
advance and spread of the broad-heads.

Were these people Celts or at least partially
celticized? To express an opinion on a Celtic
question is to accept an invitation to a Donnybrook fair. Anthropologically they differ markedly from the later Celtic invaders. But their
custom of incineration is certainly suggestive,

and it is not at all impossible that they spoke a Celtic dialect. They certainly seem to prove that the westward migration from the region of the Black Sea or from farther eastward had not ceased or been turned backward at this time. The spread of North German people southward at this time would have brought them where they would mingle with Celts coming westward and receive their first lesson in Indo-European language and culture, if it came from the east.

There is at present a strong tendency to seek the original Indo-European homeland neither in the extreme east or extreme west or north, but somewhere in the open country of southern Russia lying to the north of the Black Sea or farther eastward toward the Caspian. Here they locate them mainly in a long zone of parkland extending along the southern edge of the forest zone and in the valleys of the great rivers. Here at a much later date Scythians were settled who raised large quantities of wheat, while others were nomadic. We remember that Neolithic trade-routes followed mainly rivers and seashore. The islands of the Mediterranean were occupied early and sea commerce found a centre in Crete. A great centre of trade arose very early at Troy (Hissarlik), on the highway between the Ægean and the settlements along the shores of the Black Sea and in the valleys of the rivers descending from the interior.

Déchellette has called attention to the striking analogies in form of settlement, in primitive idols, in pottery with painting and spiral ornament between the villages of the Balkans, Troy (Hissarlik) and of the Troad and Phrygia, and of the pre-Mycenæan culture of Crete and Greece. "Between Butmir and Hissarlik these discoveries mark the routes which already undoubtedly connected pre-Hellenic peoples and pre-Celtic tribes."

Meyer tells us that the banded pottery shows the same motives in ornament in Butmir and Tordos as in Troy and the Ægean, and spreads thence northward and westward; and that painted pottery in Europe starts at the end of the Neolithic (2500–2000 B. C.) in the great plain east of the Carpathians in the region of the Dniester and Dnieper, a region of high culture in other respects. "Here the connection with the Ægean world is evident (*augenfällig*)." This people was agricultural. They burned their dead, and Meyer thinks that incineration spread northward and westward from this centre. They show no use of metal. Their cul-

ture breaks off suddenly at the end of the Neolithic period.

Here is a region which stands in free communication with the agricultural population of
the parkland zone, open to influences from the
steppe, accepting the higher civilization of
Phrygia and the Ægean. It is a people of advanced agriculture, hence probably of rapidly
increasing population, open to trade and commerce. Here wide and free communications
would be likely to prevent the formation of an
unyielding cake or crust of custom. People
meeting from all lands and cultures might well
make and use a language capable of expressing
a great variety of shades of thought peculiar to
a variety of peoples and cultures; we might
safely call it a mixed language springing from
a mixture of peoples. Here, as in the Ægean
region, the more or less fortified town or village would be a necessity. Here the horse and
wagon would be early introduced from the east.
Here the patriarchate, so characteristic of nomadic tribes, would be early imported from the
steppe, or may have been developed independently.

There is a universality in the Indo-European
religion, a sanity and proportion in their whole
mode of thought, a broad sympathy, a willing-

ness to accept new ideas and conditions — in general, a breadth of mind which could hardly be the product of isolation but rather of men who had "seen the customs of many men and many cities," and could look with tolerance and charity on alien cultures and fully appreciate their worth and advantages. Our Teutonic ancestors carried their mental and cultural environment with them wherever they went. They were apostles of purity of blood and hence of isolation. They were never good mixers, as were Celt and Achæan. All three migrated and conquered far and wide, and both usually disappeared in the alien population. But the Teuton left little impression on the alien culture, while Achæan and Celt leavened the whole mass. Here, as in other respects, Celt and Teuton show an incompatibility and oppositeness which strongly suggest difference of origin.

But we must carefully avoid too great certainty and definiteness of assertion. The weight of probability seems to be against any theory which locates the first, original homeland in the far east or in the far northwest. But we deal only with probabilities, and may well "carry our theories on our finger-tips." If the cradle was somewhere in southern Russia north of the

ARYAN

Black Sea, or somewhat farther east or west, its second homeland just before the great dispersal was vastly larger. Myres thinks that it extended far to the eastward of the Volga, which perhaps was the boundary between the eastern and western branches, and whose upper waters drained a very early home of the Finns.

The Indo-Europeans were settled in a goodly land capable with their improved agriculture of supporting a very large population. Why did they migrate in all directions? Here, again, we are left much in the dark. But Pumpelly, in his explorations at Anau, found the settlement deserted during the Bronze period about the same time when we find the Indo-Europeans leaving the homeland. At Anau there are signs that the desertion was due primarily to aridity or to disturbances accompanying such a change. It seems highly probable that climatic changes may have played a most important part in this movement, as they seem to have done in the later historical migrations from this region or from farther eastward.

We may close this chapter of uncertainties with one deduction which seems fairly evident. If the Germans were the first and original Indo-Europeans, the movement developed here directly out of preceding Neolithic conditions.

If, as seems more probable, it originated farther to the southeast, and was introduced by the Celts, or in connection with the amber trade, it made little marked interruption in the development of the Germans. They and the Scandinavians continued to take from the south whatever they would, but their development was largely independent. A complete conquest of Germany and Scandinavia by the Celts seems very improbable.

The Teutonic and Scandinavian peoples were not precocious, and appear in history very late. But here apart, in the misty northland, a people was very slowly developing who, after the decadence and fall of Rome, could come forward and slowly and wearily rebuild a civilization better than that which had fallen, and a government of, by, and for the people, guaranteeing to the individual the right of free action and development, the grandest feature of Indo-European culture. This, rather than any precocity, is the glory of the northern peoples. Once again we find history in the making in an inconspicuous people during an apparently dormant period.

He that believeth will not despise the day of small things, neither will he make haste. If the vision tarries long, he will wait for it. "It shall come and shall not tarry." It will probably come by the way which he least suspects.

There seems to be a wide-spread opinion that the rise of the Indo-Europeans was the first dawn of day in a benighted world. Their migrations were a missionary movement on a grand scale. They dispelled darkness, ignorance, and superstitions, broke the crust of a stagnant conservatism, overthrew outworn customs, brought an entirely new culture, and revolutionized life and the world. We might call attention to the fact that Indo-European culture and life were a product of Neolithic experience, that it was the blossoming of Neolithic growth, that it represented only one part or phase of Neolithic attainment. "The best traditions make the best rebels." [1] The question remains: Was Neolithic thought and feeling destroyed by their coming, or did it still persist, like a river flowing underground, and is most of our deepest life to-day a fairly direct continuation of the older current only somewhat modified by the revolution?

We notice first of all the commonness or community of Neolithic feeling and life, its almost monotonous uniformity, over Europe, eastern

[1] 375: 14.

Asia, and probably even far wider areas. We may easily exaggerate this. The cultures of the Mediterranean basin, of Spain and France, of the Danube valley, of northern Germany and Scandinavia, not to mention smaller, more isolated provinces, showed well-marked differences. There was probably more diversity in the people of every one of these provinces, especially at centres of trade, even in every larger village, than our hasty study would lead us to suspect. But in fundamental characters there was widespread and marked similarity; and this, like the wide range of dominant genera and species of animals, is a sign of vitality and fitness.

The Neolithic period coincides roughly with the latter part of Wundt's Totem Age: the Bronze period ushered in his Age of Heroes.[1] During the first period the individual counted for very little, everything was tribal. In the second period the great leaders of popular migrations emerge, young, vigorous, hot-blooded. With the appearance of these "kings of men" comes the rise of nations. Tribal control wanes, and the slow development of individual, personal judgment and conscience, self-control, and responsibility replaces it to a great extent.

We read in the history of Israel that the long

— rise of chiefdoms - rise of war.

Egyptian bondage of a stiff-necked nomad people, being broken to the rudiments of order and civilization, was followed by an exodus and a period of judges or popular leaders, when "there was no king in Israel, but every man did that which was right in his own eyes." It was a period of lawlessness and anarchy; recovery was slow and painful, and finally only partially attained by the appointment of a king. A similar education, on a vastly larger scale both of area and time, was going on all over Europe.

Prehistoric man was guided and controlled by feelings usually expressing the dictates of a long experience out of which instincts had crystallized. His feelings were his instinctive responses to new emergencies. He could not analyze them, reason or argue about them; he was spared the "malady of thought." He had little or no logic or science; his philosophy, as we have seen, was a *way* smoothed by the feet of his ancestors. He was a man of taste in the literal sense of the word. He knew what he liked and what he disliked; probably he could not have explained the reason for either feeling. He was wise in following these instinctive feelings and tastes; they represented the accumulated and assimilated experience of millennia. Of course the experience had been that of in-

dividuals. Neolithic man's school and labora-
tory of education was mostly the family and
the neighborhood. Here he had to learn to
get on with other individuals, to live and let
live, to practise co-operation and mutual aid.
Here he learned the first and grandest lessons in
morals; that he would be done by as he did,
and hence that it was best to do as he would
be done by. He has never lost or forgotten the
lessons learned in this excellent "dame's school."

Most of his higher education — and hence of
his feeling, conscience, religion, and life — was
tribal. Laws, or rather customs, were pro-
pounded by the elders of the tribe or priests,
an exceedingly conservative court. The chief
aim was not rapidity of progress, but confirm-
ing and practising that which long experience
had proved to be good. Slowly but surely the
fund of wisdom increased. "It is the three-
per-cent man who gets all the money in the
end."

Responsibility was tribal. The man who tried
experiments or "fooled" with the forbidden
thing was a common nuisance summarily and
thoroughly abated by the tribe.

Land was common property, though the individual had probably gained some rights of use.
It is doubtful whether he could use the whole

or any part of it entirely as he would. Even at a much later date his use was largely limited and controlled by ancient custom.

The ritual which still made up most of his religion was also tribal.[1] Dance and song were practised by the whole community. His creed, so far as he had one, was a belief in spiritual beings, dæmons, of great power and marvellous efficiency. Some or many were beneficent; more were probably maleficent; but those might be appeased, mollified, bribed, won over, or controlled, if rightly approached through magical rites or ceremonies.

These dæmons seem to have been supposed to be almost innumerable. No one was supreme, but some were more important than others. Here then was room for variety of opinion, of ritual, of the spirit occupying the most important place; hence also of change and development. The gods in one country were those of the hills; in another, those of the plains; in a third, of the forest. Fishing and agricultural tribes had different dæmons. The wandering trader, passing from tribe to tribe, in his own heart respected or neglected all alike. Every land had its own gods or goddesses. When a man migrated to another country he usually

[1] 293.

left his old gods at home. If he was adopted into the brotherhood of another tribe, he changed his religious allegiance also.

A religious hierarchy seems to have grown up during the Neolithic period headed by the goddess-mother of life. Her rise seems to have accompanied the introduction of agriculture, which must have brought great changes in religious ritual and belief. Dæmons who had heretofore held a high place in the fear or affection of hunting tribes gradually lost their supremacy or were neglected.

The dethronement of gods or dæmons was usually not sudden or revolutionary. The new mode of life and its accompanying cult gained ground slowly. Probably it was at first an extension or modification of some older one. The dethroned divinity long retained his hold on the fears or affections of many of the tribe. Finally he was remembered only by certain old wives in remote or isolated settlements. With the rest of the people he, or she, was fast becoming an imp, kobold, or fairy — the subject of fascinating stories, still tinged with mystery, joy, or fear, but not to be taken too seriously.

Here, apparently, is one, by no means the only, source of folk-lore and fairy-tale. Folk-lore is an exceedingly wide field and our path leads through only a little corner of it. It was the growth of millennia. It preserves for us remnants of ancient beliefs and practices, whose original meaning had been forgotten long before the birth of the story-teller. Fossil beliefs of the most widely separated ages may be found jumbled together in the same story.

It was always intended to be told to a group of sympathetic listeners or to the whole community. It is genuine literature, but when reduced to writing or cold print it chills and dies. The story-teller must feel at once the sympathy or coldness of his listeners. The substance may remain unchanged, but the shading and emphasis must vary with the feeling and temper of the audience. Thus in a very true sense it was moulded by the people. If a story survived with certain forms and content, it was because it was essentially common and human, appealing to that which is not individual but at least tribal or racial.

Says Mr. Chesterton: "Our modern novels, which deal with men as they are, are chiefly produced by a small and educated section of the society. But this other literature (the kind now called folk-lore, the literature of the people) deals with men greater than they are — with demigods and heroes — and that is far too important a matter to be trusted to the educated classes. The fashioning of these portents is a popular trade, like ploughing or bricklaying; the men who made bridges, the men who made ditches, were the men who made deities. Men could not elect their kings, but they could elect their gods. So we find ourselves faced with a fundamental contrast between what is called fiction and what is called folk-lore. The one exhibits an abnormal degree of dexterity, operating within our daily limitations; the other exhibits quite normal desires extended beyond those limitations. Fiction means the common things as seen by the uncommon people. Fairy-tales mean the uncommon things as seen by the common people.

"As our world advances through history toward its present epoch, its becomes more specialist, less democratic, and folk-lore turns gradually into fiction. But it is only slowly that the old elfin fire fades into the light of common realism. For ages after our characters have dressed up in the clothes of mortals they betray the blood of the gods."[1]

The charm and wisdom of folk-lore and fairy-tale are mostly due to the commonness, in the best sense, of their subject, thought, and feeling.

[1] 376: 67; 377: 177; cf. 378.

They suit all times and places, and are immortal and timeless like their heroes. When we attempt to reclothe them in modern form or language to suit "private interpretation" their strength is departed from them.

Neolithic feeling, belief, ritual, religion; its music, art, and literature; its customs, institutions, morals, ways, and life — all these sprang from the life and experience of the tribe or community. They were essentially growths in and from the mass of the people, usually owing comparatively little to the genius of any individual inventor or discoverer. We have called them Neolithic, but some or many of them were old far back in Paleolithic time. Like the tree Ygdrasil their roots lay hold on the foundations of the world.

So deeply rooted a growth or culture is almost ineradicable, though it has a marvellous adaptability and possibilities of growth and modification. It could never have been destroyed by its own Indo-European children, however rebellious. It must survive somewhere though probably changed for the better. We have found reasons to doubt whether Roman capacity for discipline and government, Roman laws and institutions, were predominantly of Indo-European origin. We were still more doubtful whether the glory of Teutonic or Scandinavian history is due to its being Indo-European, or whether it was the result of a continuous, unbroken development from Neolithic times. If ever any culture seems largely native and indigenous, responsive to outside influences but always retaining its independent self-determination and power of selection and choice as to what and how far it will assimilate, that culture is to be found in northern Germany and Scandinavia.

We have seen the fate of Olympian religion and Achæan thought in Greece. The Achæans were a small minority completely outnumbered by an exceedingly conservative native population. They were absorbed and became a part of the Greek people, and their contribution must not be underestimated. We have noted the marvellous vitality of the old Neolithic thought, its re-emergence, its influence on Greek philosophy. We remember that the great seat of progress was not in Dorian Sparta but in "Pelasgic Athens," almost unknown to Homer.

The Celt was, if anything, a better "mixer" and more adaptable than even the Achæan. His prejudices and zeal in regard to morals and religion seem not to have been deep or strong. The Celts were finally absorbed, affecting the temper of the people far more than their daily life.

Through all these revolutions, as well as those which were to follow, family and neighborhood retained their compact unity, perhaps with all its mutual attractions strengthened by the pressure of the conquerors. They were still the controlling influence in the life and education of the individual, as they probably remain to this day. The power of these smaller communities may have waxed, as tribal control waned. What they had lost in the mutual support within the tribe they made good by leaning more closely on their neighbors.

This solidarity makes the common people very stiff-necked, in an excellent sense of the word. Like the Neolithic folk of Scandinavia, they select and accept from their more cultured neighbors only that which they can assimilate to the stores of experience and instincts which they already possess. The fickleness, of which they are often accused, is characteristic of a very different class or stratum of the population, and of far later origin and development. Their own development is naturally slow, gradual, and continuous.

We have ventured the opinion that the essentials of Neolithic culture survived the conquests of the Indo-Europeans in a but slightly modified form. If this is granted, we have every reason to think that the effects of all succeeding invasions and conquests, changes of dynasties and governments, international or national policies, internal legislation and reforms, have been even more temporary, slight, and superficial. Modern revolutions have been more and more uprisings of the people asserting the inalienable rights and privileges of their dignity as men. The trend of popular life and feeling has resembled the flow of a river or the incoming of the tide. It turns or winds as it meets obstacles in its path, but keeps in the main to a fairly clear course and direction. The people may not be against the government, they merely go their way regardless of it. But we must not trespass on the field of the historian.

During the Neolithic period everybody, except perhaps certain priests and elders, belonged to the common people. But accumulation of wealth, the rise of leaders, the conquest of new lands developed a distinct aristocracy of birth, wealth, prowess, leadership, and genius. The common people of to-day, whom, as Mr. Lincoln said, "God must have loved or he never would have made so many of them," seem to be the whole population minus the uncommon aristocracy. It is not easy to see just where we ought to draw the line between mass and class.

All the virtues, brains, and possibilities of progress can hardly be confined to this upper stratum. Can we define or describe our common people? They are a very mixed multitude. There is probably more individual variety than among the conventional refined and cultured, and this makes them more original and interesting. Hence any composite picture is usually a blur; a definite picture of any group or part would be partial and one-sided, very possibly a caricature of the whole. We dare not try to offer one.

Men and women like Mr. Robert Woods, of Boston, and Miss Jane Addams, of Chicago, have set themselves patiently, persistently, sympathetically, respectfully, and wisely to study and help these people. They can and will describe them, if we will listen. Their faith in the people seems to be deep and strong.

We all recognize that in times of trial and emergency, when great testing moral issues are at stake, the people are practically unanimous in recognizing and supporting the cause of justice and right, unless befogged, divided, or misled by statesmen. Their taste for right ends is keen and reliable. Their feelings ring true, and they act accordingly, whatever the cost.

They are not inarticulate, though their speech is often interjectory. They are only beginning to produce a large number of spokesmen. Now and then their demands are voiced by a prophet, asserting that what Jehovah demands is "to do justly, to love mercy, and to walk humbly with thy God"; or the prophecy is sung by a poet, like Burns. They may sometimes or often be misled; but if their heart and feeling is not healthy we may well despair of the republic.

But the true prophet is very rarely a statesman. His feeling and taste for ends is marvellously good. Here his word, like the feeling of the people from whom he sprang, is almost infallible. But the choice of means and policy, the selection of the next step toward the attainment of the end, is the real business of the statesman.

The *élite* of wealth, learning, and culture to-day have generally given up the search for ends in life. The old question: "What is man's chief end?" sounds archaic. We are doubtful as to the existence or desirability of such a thing. We are, in the language of the broker, very "long" on means, but terribly "short" on ends, for which there is no market. Some day we shall again find a place for end and purpose in our philosophy and science, as in the systems of Paul, Plato, and especially of Aristotle, with his "passion for the obvious," but at present these thinkers are back numbers. Yet we must have ends of life beyond mere survival, comfort, or luxury, and getting a living. Some scale of values, not solely and purely mercantile, would also be useful.

If the aristocracy of wealth, learning, and culture can provide us no adequate system of ends and values in life, would it not be well for us to borrow temporarily a few from the people? Might we not to good advantage even go into partnership with them, cordially accepting their ends, and loyally and honestly attempting to find the means of attaining them? The result might be a solidarity of thought, feeling, action, and final attainment superior even to those of our Neolithic ancestors.

You may possibly say: "We in America are already living under a democratic form of government — 'of the people, by the people, and for the people.'" Is this the statement of an accomplished fact or the definition of a dim, far-off event toward which we hope we are moving?

How far did the framers of our Constitution desire or intend that the will of the people should govern? Was the method of choosing and electing the President of the United States, as originally devised, intended to make that election popular or not? We have changed that. Did they intend that the Senate of the United States should be a means of carrying out the will of the people, or rather that it should defer or check its becoming the law of the land? Does our governmental action to-day represent the will of the people? Is it truly representative?

Perhaps our ancestors were wise in their caution. Perhaps a change has become advisable. We are asking how far government changes or modifies the people; how far governmental action, change of President or controlling party, their legislation and policies, affect the deeper currents of character and life. The people seem to me to be still continuing to go their own way and to follow quietly but firmly their own line of development, largely regardless of the votes of national Congress or State legislature, perhaps sometimes with a slight sigh of relief at their adjournment. It may be best that it is so. The independence and continuity of popular development is still maintained to-day as throughout prehistoric times.

How far do our vast accumulations of learning and discovery, our deep or superficial systems of philosophy, our splendid or decadent *fin de siècle* art and literature reach and affect these people? Their chief characteristic is an attempt at distinction, an artificial uncommonness, a self-consciousness entirely foreign to the thinker of the common mind.

The institution which has the widest and deepest influence on their feeling, thought, and life is the church. They generally love it, for they are "incurably religious." It is conservative in the best sense of the word. It represents, of course imperfectly, the feelings, aspirations, and hopes of all men everywhere in all ages — in one word, of humanity. It stands for the worth, dignity, and brotherhood of man, and the fatherhood of God. It is almost alone to-day in recognizing that there are ends in life. It offers a way of progress and a reasonable ground of hope in a somewhat weary age inclined to indulge in criticism, fault-finding, and pessimism. The fact that it is generally roundly abused for its defects, mistakes, and sins of omission, for its inability to accomplish the impossible, is a sign of the great hope and confidence which we have rightly reposed in it.

The discordant chorus of mutually destructive criticisms arising from the cultured and intellectual classes seems to show that it is following fairly well a straight, right, and wise course, as Mr. Lincoln is said to have suggested concerning his own experience, plans, and leadership in a similar situation. "Wisdom is justified of her children," but the families of the elect are small. That the church does not conform to all the theories — not to say vagaries and fads — of to-day is no discredit. Most of them will be very unfashionable to-morrow. "The fashion of this age passeth away."

The existence of our nation evidently depends far more upon the fundamental and essential, nay obvious, old and common human virtues of very common people than upon our art and learning, the shrewdness of our politicians and profiteers, the amount of our wealth and exports, our inventions or luxuries, the winning of an election, or the defeat of any party. In one word, which we have already repeated *ad nauseam*, our chief business to-day is to continue the line of development clearly marked out by our benighted ancestors of prehistoric days — to exercise, develop, and strengthen the best instincts and feelings crystallized out of millennia of experience; to see to it that they are expressed in the law and practices of the land and commonwealth; and that they are not smothered under a mass of inventions of yesterday and of conventions of to-day. The fact that all this is entirely obvious should not conceal its importance.

The old message comes to us: "If thou altogether holdest thy peace at this time, then shall there enlargement and deliverance arise from another place; but thou and thy father's house shall be destroyed; and who knoweth whether thou art come to the kingdom for such a time as this?"

In the northern ocean we see icebergs moving slowly southward. They are not driven by the winds which to-day are blowing against their broad fronts. The most conspicuous feature of our field of vision is the white foam capping the waves. To-morrow it will be blown away, evaporate, and disappear in the shifting winds which have tossed it into view. The berg is carried by the great polar current, silent, inconspicuous, irresistible, unchanging in its course, guided by still deeper and more ancient and permanent cosmic forces.

We know something about oceanic currents. Of the current of the evolution of life we know almost nothing; but hope that our theories are no more inadequate than the feelings of our

Neolithic ancestors.   Certainly the current has not yet been charted.   We catch glimpses of the direction of its sweep.   Over what stormy and dangerous seas and to what undiscovered island or continent it is carrying us we do not know.   It seems to set toward fairer climes beyond our vision.   We set sail millions of years ago; we shall not arrive to-morrow.

BIBLIOGRAPHY

A FEW SUGGESTIONS

The first series of books referred to in the following lists (A–O) are general, and every one covers a large field. The works of Déchelette and Hoernes (A and B) contain a very rich bibliography down to 1907 or 1908. They should be carefully studied first of all; afterward the remainder of the list. I have omitted from the following list many excellent articles to which they refer. This list will satisfy the needs of the ordinary reader.

The second list (1–378) contains references to articles or books on special subjects which I have been obliged to treat very briefly in this small book. These will introduce the reader to other writers on the same subject. He is urged to make his own bibliography, and will find that he has started on an endless chain of most fascinating research, for which I hope he may form an insatiable appetite.

The following list of abbreviations and corresponding complete titles may save the reader some inconvenience. In this connection he may well consult the Introduction to Déchelette's *Manuel* (A) I, pp. xv–xix.

Amer. Nat.............*American Naturalist.*
Amer. Anth...........*American Anthropologist.*
Sci. Mo...............*Science Monthly.* (Continuation of *Popular Science Monthly.*)
A. f. A. (Arch. f. Anth.)..*Archiv für Anthropologie.*
Zts. f. Eth............*Zeitschrift für Ethnologie.*
L'Anth................*L'Anthropologie.*
R. E. A...............*Revue d'école d'Anthropologie*, Paris.
Rev. Arch............*Revue Archéologique.*
Korr.-bl. d. d. Ges......*Korrespondenz-blatt der deutschen Gesellschaft für Anthropologie.*
Cong. Int.............*Congrès international d'Anthropologie et d'Archéologie.*

GENERAL

A. Déchelette, J. *Manuel d'Archéologie Préhistorique.* Paris, 1908. 3 vols. Vol. I. *Archéologie Préhistorique.*

B. Hoernes, M. *Natur- und Urgeschichte des Menschen.* Vienna, 1909. 2 vols.

C. —— *Urgeschichte des Menschen,* Vienna, 1892.

D. Obermaier, H. *Der Mensch aller Zeiten.* Berlin, 1911–12. Vol. I. *Der Mensch der Vorzeit.*

E. Forrer, R. *Urgeschichte des Europäers.* Stuttgart, 1908.

F. —— *Reallexikon der prähistorischen, klassichen und frühchristlichen Alterthümer.* Stuttgart, 1907–08.

G. Müller, S. *Nordische Alterthumskunde* (trans. Jiriczek). Strassburg, 1897. Vol. I. *Steinzeit–Bronzezeit.*

H. —— *Urgeschichte Europas* (trans. Jiriczek). Strassburg, 1905.

I. —— *L'Europe préhistorique* (trans. Philipot). Paris, 1907.

J. Montelius, O. *Kulturgeschichte Schwedens.* Leipsic, 1906.

K. —— *Les Temps préhistoriques en Suède* (trans. Reinach). Paris, 1895.

L. Avebury, Lord (Sir John Lubbock). *Prehistoric Times.* New York, 1913.

M. Elliot, G. F. S. *Prehistoric Man and His Story.* London, 1915.

N. Schwantes, G. *Aus Deutschland's Urzeit.* Leipsic, 1913.

O. Wundt, W. *Elements of Folk Psychology* (trans. Schaub, E. L.). London, 1915.

CHAPTER I—THE COMING OF MAN

1. Lull, R. S. *Organic Evolution.* New York, 1917.

2. Wilder, H. H. *History of the Human Body.* New York, 1909.

3. Cope, E. D. *Primary Factors of Evolution.* Chicago, 1895, p. 150.

5. Osborn, H. F. *Age of Mammals.* New York, 1910.

6. Loomis, F. B. "Adaptation of Primates," *Amer. Nat.,* XLV, 1911, 479.

7. Gregory, W. K. "Studies in the Evolution of Primates," *Bull. Amer. Mus. Nat. Hist.*, XXV, 1916, Art. XIX, 239.

8. Barrell, J. "Probable Relations of Climatic Changes to Origin of Tertiary Ape-Man," *Sci. Mo.*, N. S., IV, 1917, 16.

9. Matthew, W. D. "Climate and Evolution," *Ann. N. Y. Acad. Sci.*, XXIV, 1915, 170.

10. Pilgrim, G. E. "New Siwalik Primates," *Records of Geol. Survey of India*, XLIII, 1913, Part IV, 264.

11. Chamberlain, T. C., and Salisbury, R. D. *Geology.* New York, 1904, Vol. III, 534.

12. Lydekker, L. K. *Geographical History of Mammals.* Cambridge, 1896, 201, 265, 288, 334.

13. Pirsson, L. V., and Schuchert, C. *Text-Book of Geology.* New York, 1915, Part II, 925, 948, 964, 976.

14. Smith, G. E. *Presidential Address*, Brit. Assoc. Adv. Sci. Dundee, 1912, 575.

15. Heinemann, T. W. *Physical Basis of Civilization.* Chicago, 1908.

16. Fiske, J. *Destiny of Man.* Boston, 1884.

17. Drummond, H. *Ascent of Man.* New York, 1894.

18. Kropotkin, P. A. *Mutual Aid a Factor in Evolution.* New York, 1903.

19. Jones, F. W. *Arboreal Man.* New York and London, 1916.

PITHECANTHROPUS

See A, I, 273; B, I, 181; D, I, 370; 40, 73.

24. Du Bois, E. *Smithson. Report*, 1897–98, 445.

25. Berry, E. W. "Environment of Ape-Man," *Sci. Mo.*, N. S., III, 1906, 161.

26. Keith, A. *Ancient Types of Man.* New York, 1911.

PRIMITIVE HUMAN MIGRATIONS

30. Keane, A. H. *Ethnology.* Cambridge, 1901.

31. Deniker, J. *Races of Man.* London, 1900.

32. Haddon, A. C. *The Wanderings of Peoples.* Cambridge, 1911.

33. —— *Races of Man and Their Distribution.* New York, 1910.

MAN'S ARRIVAL IN EUROPE

40. Osborn, H. F.   *Men of the Old Stone Age.*   New York, 1915.

41. Ranke, J.   *Der Mensch.*   Leipsic, 1900.

42. Geikie, J.   *Antiquity of Man in Europe.*   Edinburgh, 1914.

43. —— *The Great Ice Age.*   3d ed.   London, 1894.

44. Reinhardt, L.   *Der Mensch zur Eiszeit in Europa.*   Munich, 1906.

45. Geikie, J.   "Tundras and Steppes of Prehistoric Europe," *Smithson. Report*, 1897–98, 321.

46. Nehring, A.   *Tundren u. Steppen der Jetzt- und Vor-zeit.* Berlin, 1890.

47. Schöetensack, O.   *Der Unterkiefer des "Homo Heidelbergensis."* Leipsic, 1908.

48. MacCurdy, G. G.   "The Eolith Problem," *Amer. Anth.*, N. S., VII, 1905, 425.

49. Sollas, W. J.   *Ancient Hunters.*   2d ed.   London, 1915.

60. Hoops, J.   *Waldbäume und Kulturpflanzen, im german. Alterthum.*   Strassburg, 1905.

Danish Shell-heaps.   See **D**, 465–476; **G**, **I**, 4; **L**, 226.

61. Steenstrup, J.   *Arch. f. Anth.*, XIX, 1891, 361.

62. Sarauw, F. C.   "Maglemose," *Prähist. Zeits.*, III, 1911, 52; VI, 1914, 1.

63. Virchow, R.   "Rinnekalns," *Korresp.-blatt. der deutschen Ges. f. Anthrop.*, XXVIII, 1897, 147.

64. Ebert, M.   "Die baltischen Provinzen," *Prähist. Zeits.*, V, 1913, 498; Mugem, **C**, 232.

65. Cartailhac, E.   *Ages préhistoriques de l'Espagne et du Portugal*, p. 48.

66. Munro, R.   *Palæolithic Man and Terramara Settlements in Europe.*   New York, 1912.

67. Morlot, A.   *Société Vandoise des Sci. Nat.*, VI, No. 46. "Etudes géologico-archéologiques."   (Shell-heaps and Lake-dwellings.)   Lausanne, 1860.

CHAPTER III—LAND HABITATIONS
CAVE-DWELLINGS

B, 31; **C**, 258; **E**, 120, 139.

75. Dawkins, W. B.   *Cave Hunting.*   London, 1874.

76. Fraipont, J.   *Les Cavernes et leurs Habitants.*   Paris, 1896.

HUTS AND VILLAGES

B, 51, 65, 84.

80. Montelius, O. "Zur ältesten Geschichte des Wohnhauses in Europa," *Arch. f. Anth.*, XXIII, 1895, 451. Cf. H, 25, 68; J, 15.

81. Schliz, A. "Der Bau vorgeschichtlicher Wohnanlagen," *Mitt. d. Anth. Ges. Wien*, 1903, 301.

82. Castelfranco, P. "Les Fonds des Cabanes," *Rev. d'Anth.*, XVI, 1887, 182. Cf. A, 347, 350; E, 139.

83. Schliz, A. *Das steinzeitliche Dorf Grosgartach.* Stuttgart, 1901.
    Rev. Virchow, R., *Arch. f. Anth.*, XXVII, 1892, 435.
    Rev. Reinach, S., *L'Anth.*, XII, 1901, 704.

84. Possler, W. "Die Abarten des Altsächsischen Bauernhauses," *Arch. f. Anth.*, XXXVI, 1909, 157.

85. Mielke, R. "Entwickelungsgeschichte der sächsischen Hausform," *Zts. f. Eth.*, XXXV, 1903, 509.

CHAPTER IV—LAKE-DWELLINGS

90. Munro, R. *Lake Dwellings of Europe.* London, 1890. Full Bibliography until 1890.
    See also L, 180; A, 363; E, 158; B, 98; C, 234; D, 515.

91. Keller, F. *Lake Dwellings of Switzerland.* 2d ed. London, 1878.

92. Troyon, F. *Habitations lacustres du Lac de Neuchâtel.* Paris, 1865.

93. Gross, V. *Les Protohelvéites.* Paris, 1883.

94. Schuhmacher. *Arch. f. Anth.*, N. F., VII, 1903, 254.

95. Heierlei, J. *Urgeschichte der Schweiz.* Zurich, 1901.

96. Schenk, A. *La Suisse Préhistorique.* Lausanne, 1912.

97. Bölsche, W. *Mensch der Pfahlbauzeit.* 8th ed. Stuttgart, 1911.

98. Heer, O. *Die Pflanzen der Pfahlbauten*, 1886. See 91, I, 518.
    Cf. 60.

CHAPTER V—A GLANCE EASTWARD

110. Pumpelly, R. *Explorations in Turkestan*, Carnegie Inst. Pub., Washington, No. 73, 1904, 2 vols., vol. I, p. 50, chaps. I, III, V.

111. Rev. by Schmidt, H. *Prähist. Zeits.*, I, 1909–10, 413.

112. Capitan, L. "L'Histoire d'Élam," *Rev. d'éc. d'Anth.*, XII, 1902, 187.

113. Düssaud, R. "Anciennes Civilisations orientales," *Rev. d'éc. d'Anth.*, XVII, 1907, 97.

114. Schrader, Fr. "Questions d'Orient," *Rev. d'éc. d'Anth.*, XVIII, 1908, 267; XX, 1910, 73.

115. Delitzsch, F. *Rep. Smithson. Inst.*, 1900, 535.

116. Morgan, J. de. *Premières Civilisations*. Paris, 1909.

117. *Mémoires de la Delegation en Perse*, I, 1900, 181–190 (Susa).

118. *Mémoires de la Delegation en Perse I* (Tepeh Moussian), VIII, 1906. Cf. B, II, 168.

119. Morgan, J. de. "Les Ages de la Pierre dans l'Asie mineure," *Bull. Soc. d'Anth.* Paris, Ser. V, III, 1902, 708.

121. King, L. W. *History of Babylonia and Assyria*, Part I. New York, 1910.

122. Sayce, A. H. *Archæology of Cuneiform Inscriptions*. London, 1907, 67–100.

123. Hall, H. R. "Discoveries in Crete, and Their Relations to Palestine and Egypt," *Proc. Soc. Bib. Arch.*, XXXI, 1909, 311.

124. Myres, J. L. *Dawn of History*. New York, 1911, 121, 202.

125. Breasted, J. H. *Ancient Times*. New York, 1914, 100.

ORIGIN OF AGRICULTURE AND CATTLE-RAISING

See **B, I**, 535–591; **M**, chaps. XII, XIII.

135. Reinhardt, L. *Die Erde und die Kultur*. Munich, 1912 (?).
    a. Vol. I, *Die Erde und ihr Wirthschaftsleben*.
    b. Vol. II, *Kulturgeschichte des Menschen*.
    c. Vol. III, *Kulturgeschichte der Nutzthiere*.
    d. Vol. IV, *Kulturgeschichte der Pflanzen*.

136. *La Grande Encycl.*, Art. "Agriculture."

137. Hehn, V. *Kulturpflanzen und Hausthiere.* Berlin, 1911.
138. Mason, O. T. *Woman's Share in Primitive Culture.* New York, 1907, 146, chap. II.
139. Buschan, G. "Heimat und Alter der europäischen Kulturpflanzen," *Korr.-bl. d. d. Ges.*, XVIII, 1889, 128.
140. Roth. "Origin of Agriculture," *Journ. Anth. Inst.*, XVI, 102.
141. Zaborowski, M. S. "Le Blé en Asie et en Europe," *Rev. d'éc. d'Anth.*, XVI, 1906, 359.
142. Much, M. "Vorgeschichtliche Nähr- und Nutz-Pflanzen in Europa," *Mitt. Anth. Ges. Wien*, XXXVIII, 1908, 195 ff. Favors European origins.

CHAPTER VI—MEGALITHS

See A, I, chap. III; B, II, 440; D, 500; G, chap. V; J, 43; L, chap. V.

150. Peet, T. E. *Rude Stone Monuments and Their Builders.* New York, 1912.
151. Windle, B. C. A. *Remains of Prehistoric Age in England.* London, 1904.
152. Krause, E., und Schötensack, O. "Die megalithischen Gräber Deutschlands," *Zts. f. Eth.*, XXV, 1893, 105.
153. Lienau, M. M. "Megalithgräber u. sonstige Grabformen der Lüneburger Gegend," *Mannusbib.*, XIII, 1914.
154. Montelius, O. *Orient und Europa.* Stockholm, 1899.
155. Wilke, G. "Sudwesteurop. Megalithkultur," *Mannusbib.* VII.
156. Hermet (Abbé), "Statues-Menhirs," *L'Anth.*, XII, 1901, 595.
157. Cartailhac, E. *La France Préhistorique.* Paris, 1889.

DISPOSAL OF DEAD

164. Helm, K. *Altgermanische Religionsgeschichte.* Heidelberg, 1913, 132, *Bib.*
165. Schliz, A. "Steinzeitliche Bestattungsformen in Südwestdeutschland," *Korr.-bl. d. d. Ges.*, XXXII, 1901, 60.
166. Andrée, R. "Hockerbestattung und Ethnologie," *A. f. A.*, XXXIV, 1907, 282, 303.

167. Schötensack, O. "Bedeutung der Hockerbestattung," *Zts. f. Eth.*, XXXIII, 1901, 522.

168. Götze, A. "Ueber Hockergräber," *Korr.-bl. d. d. Ges.*, 1899, 321.

169. Olshausen, O. "Leichenverbrennung," *Zts. f. Eth.*, 1892, 129.

170. Seger, H. "Entstehung der Leichenverbrennung," *Korr.-bl. d. d. Ges.*, XLI, 1910, 115.

CHAPTER VII—NEOLITHIC INDUSTRIES

179. Veblen, T. *The Instinct of Workmanship.* New York, 1914.

   Clothing. G, I, 268; J, 19; **90**, F.

   Ornaments. B, II, 328; A, II, 570.

   Implements. A, 513; B, II, 168; D, 472, 478; E, **178**; F, Art. "Axt"; G, 22; **46**, 133; J, 24.

   Salt. B, II, 23, 89; F, Art. "Salz"; N, 114.

   Gold. A, 627; B, II, 207; C, 320.

   Copper. A, II; B, II, 546; D, 494, 499, 545; E, 278.

180. Much, M. *Die Kupferzeit in Europa.* 2 Auf. Jena, 1893.

181. Hampel, J. "Neue Studien über die Kupferzeit," *Zts. f. Eth.*, XXVIII, 1896, 57.

182. Montelius, O. "Die Chronologie der ältesten Bronzezeit," *Arch. f. Anth.*, XXV, 443; XXVI.

   Ships, rock-carvings of. J, 126; C, 389; G, 466; E, 347.

   Nephrite and Jadeite. A, I, 519, 573; B, II, 504; D, 510; **95**, 116; **96**, Index.

185. Mehlis, C. "Exotische Steinbeile der neol. Zeit," *Arch. f. Anth.*, XXVII, 1902, 519.

186. Peet, T. E. *Stone and Bronze Ages of Italy.* Oxford, 1909.

   Amber. A, 623; B, I, 513; II, 345, 353; D, 556; G, I, 52.

   Trade. B, II, 466–529; A, I, 619; **228**; **154**.

   Pottery. A, 547; D, 481; **116**, 195–207; F, Art. "Gefässe," **95**, 184.

190. Hoernes, M. "Die neol. Keramik in Oestreich," *Zts. f. Eth.*, 1903, 438.

191. Smith, R. A. "Development of Neolithic Pottery," *Archæologia*, LXII, 340.

192. Meyer, E. *Geschichte des Alterthums*, II, 824. 2d ed. Stuttgart, 1909.

193. Schuchhardt, C. "Das technische Element in den Anfängen der Kunst," *Prähist. Zeits.*, I, 37.

194. Verworn, M. *Kulturkries der Bandkeramik*. II, 145.

195. Reche, O. "Zur Anthropologie der jüngeren Steinzeit in Böhmen," *Arch. f. Anth.*, XXXV, 1908, 220.

196. Seger, H. "Steinzeit in Schlesien," *Arch. f. Anth.*, N. F. V., 1906.

197. Götze, A. "Neolithische Kugelamphoren," *Zts. f. Eth.*, XXXII, 154, 1900.

198. —— "Eintheilung der neol. Periode in Mitteleuropa," *Korr.-bl. d. d. Ges.*, XXXI, 1900, 133.

199. Schuchhardt, C. "Neol. Häuser bei Lissdorf," *Zts. f. Eth.*, XLIII, 1911, 998.

200. Wosinsky, M. *Die inkrustierte Keramik*. Berlin, 1904.

201. Closmadeuc, G. de. "La Céramique dans les Dolmens de Morbihan," *Rev. Arch.*, I, 257.

202. Schmidt, H. "Vorgeschichte Spaniens," *Zts. f. Eth.*, XLV, 238, 1913.

203. Volkow, Th. "L'Industrie prémycénienne des Stations néolithiques de l'Ukraine," *L'Anth.*, XIII, 1902, 57.

204. Zaborowski, M. S. "Industrie Égéenne sur le Dnieper et le Dniester," *Bull. Soc. Anth.*, Paris, 1900, 481.

CHAPTER VIII—NEOLITHIC CHRONOLOGY

214. Menzel, H. "Geologische Entwickelungsgeschichte der älteren Postglacialzeit," *Zts. f. Eth.*, XLVI, 1914, 206–240.

215. Montelius, O. "Chronologie der jüngeren Steinzeit in Skandinavien," *Korr.-bl. d. d. Ges.*, XXII, 1891, 99–105.

216. —— "Chronologie der ältesten Bronzezeit," *Arch. f. Anth.*, XXVI, 1899, 905.

217. —— "Preclassical Chronology of Greece and Italy," *Journ. Anth. Inst.*, 1897.

302 BIBLIOGRAPHY

218. —— "Chronologie préhistorique," *Cong. Int. d'Anth. et d'Arch.*, XII, 339. Cf. Muller, S. Ibid, X. Paris, 228.

219. Scheitelig, H. "Vorgeschichte Norwegens," *Mannus.*, III, 1911, 29.

220. Kossina, G. "Urfinnen und Urgermanen," *Mannus.*, I, 17.

221. Worsaae, J. J. A. "Arctic Cultures," *Cong. Int. d'Anth. et d'Arch.* Stockholm, VII, 1874, 208.
Also, J, 63; M, 317 and *Bib.*, 323.

222. Types of Axe, G, I, 48; B, II, 184; A, I, 334; F, Art. "Aexte." Cf. also "Zeitalter."

223. Montelius, O. "Les differents Types des Haches," *Cong. Int. d'Anth. et d'Arch.* Stockholm, VII, I, 238.

226. Schmidt, R. R. "Die Grundlagen für die Diluviale Chronologie u. Paläethnologie Westeuropas," *Zts. f. Eth.*, XLIII, 1911, 945. Cf. *Korr.-bl. d. d. Ges.*, XLI, 1910.

227. Holst. "Commencement et Fin de la Période Glacieuse," *L'Anth.*, XXIV, 1913, 353.

228. Wilke, G. "Kulturbeziehungen zwischen Indien, Orient und Europa," *Mannusbibliothek*, X, 1913.

229. Schmidt, H. "Troja, Mykene, Ungarn," *Zts. f. Eth.*, XXXVI, 1904, 608, 645.

230. Anthes, E. "Alte und neue steinzeitliche Funde aus Hessen," *Prähist. Zeits.*, II, 1910, 60.

CHAPTER IX—NEOLITHIC PEOPLES AND THEIR MIGRATIONS

ATLASES

240. Bartholemew, J. G. *Advanced Atlas of Physical and Political Geography.* London, 1917.

241. —— *International Student's Atlas.* London, ——?

242. See **40**, 489; **457** and **278**, 261, 300, 500; B, I, 241, 268–360; *Bib.* E, 256; J, 57; M, chaps. X–XIV, 211; *Bib.* **49**, 435.

243. Breuil, L'Abbé, H. "Les Subdivisions du Paléolithique supérieur et leur Signification," *Cong. Int. d'Anth. et d'Arch.* Session XIV, Genève, 1912, 165.

BIBLIOGRAPHY 303

244. Sergi, G. *The Mediterranean Race*, London, 1901, chaps. II, X, 40.
245. Myres, J. L. Essay II, 51–54, in Marvin, F. S. *The Unity of Western Civilization.*
246. Ripley, W. L. *The Races of Europe.* New York, 1899.
247. Deniker, J. "Les Races Européennes," *Journ. Anth. Inst.*, XXIV.
—— "Les six Races composant la Population de l'Europe," *ibid.*
250. Schliz, A. "Vorgeschichtliche Schadeltypen deutschen Länder," *Arch. f. Anth.*, XXXVI (N. F. IX), 1910, 239. Cf. B, II, 101.
251. —— "Beiträge zur prähistorischen Ethnologie," *Prähist. Zeits.*, IV, 1912, 36.
252. —— "Bedeutung der somatischen Anthropologie," *Korr.-bl. d. d. Ges.*, XL, 1909, 66.
253. —— "Vorstufen der Nordisch-europäischen Schädelbildung," *Arch. f. Anth.*, XLI, 1914, 169.
254. —— "Der schnurkeramische Kulturkreis," *Zts. f. Eth.*, XXXVIII, 1906, 312.
260. Reche, O. "Zur Anthropologie der jüngeren Steinzeit in Schlesien und Böhmen," *Arch. f. Anth.*, 1908.
261. See 351.
262. Klassen, K. *Die Völker, Europas zur jüngeren Steinzeit.* Stuttgart, 1912, *Bib.*
263. Fleure, H. J. *Human Geography in Western Europe.* London, 1918.
264. Montelius, O. "Die Einwanderung unserer Vorfahrer im Norden," *Arch. f. Anth.*, XVII, 151.
265. ——"Sur les Tombeaux et la Topographie de la Suède pendant l'âge de pierre," *Cong. Int. d'Anth. et d'Arch.*, Session VII, Stockholm, I, 74.
266. Virchow, R. "Altnordische Schädel zu Kopenhagen," *Arch. f. Anth.*, 1870.
—— "Die ältesten Einwohner von Nordeuropa," *Arch. f. Anth.*, XXV, 1898, 88.
267. Arbo, C. O. E. "Anthropo-ethnologie des Südwestnorwegens," *Arch. f. Anth.*, XXXI, 1905, 313.

268. Herve, G. "L'Ethnographie des populations françaises," *R. E. A.*, VI, 1896, 97.

269. —— "Les brachycephales néolithiques," *Rev. Ec. An.*, IV, 1894, 393; V, 1895, 18.

270. Hamy, E. T. "L'Anthropologie de Nord-France," *L'Anth.*, XIX, 1908, 46.

271. Bloch, A. "Origines des brachycephales en France," *L'Anth.*, XII, 1901, 541.

272. Luschan, F. von. "Beziehung zwischen der Alpinen Bevölkerung und den Vorderasiaten," *Korr.-bl. d. d. Ges.*, XLIV, 1915, 118.

272a. A, 482; B, 298–303; **246.**

273. Studer, T. H., und Bannwarth, E. *Crania Helvetica antiqua.* Leipsic, 1894. Reviewed *R. E. A.*, IV, 1894, 410.

274. Hervé, G. "Les populations lacustres," *R. E. A.*, V, 1895, 137.

FOR EFFECTS OF GEOGRAPHIC ENVIRONMENT

275. Ratzel. *Anthropogeographie.* 3te Auf. Stuttgart, 1909.

276. Semple, E. *Influences of Geographical Environment.* New York.

277. Demolins, E. *Les Français d'Aujourd'hui.* Paris, 1898.

278. —— *Les grandes Routes des Peuples.* Paris, 1901.

CHAPTER X—NEOLITHIC RELIGION

290. Huxley, T. H. *Science and Education*, Essays. New York, 1897, p. 85.

291. —— *Method and Results*, Essays. New York, 1901. Essay I, p. 18.

292. Goethe, J. W. *Gedichte, Das Göttliche.*

293. Harrison, J. E. *Ancient Art and Ritual.* New York, 1913.

294. Smith, W. R. *Religion of the Semites.* Edinburgh, 1889. Origin of Religion. See **O**, 75.

295. Durkeim, E. *Elementary Forms of the Religious Life.* Trans. J. W. Swain, London, *Bib.*

BIBLIOGRAPHY 305

296. Tylor, E. B. *Primitive Culture.* 4th ed. New York, 1903.
297. —— *Anthropology.* New York, 1916.
298. Frazer, J. G. *The Golden Bough.* 3d ed. London, 1914, *Bib.* '
299. Müller, F. M. *Origin and Growth of Religion.* New York, 1879.
300. Bagehot, W. *Physics and Politics.* New York and London.
301. Montgomery, J. E. (Editor). *Religions of the Past and Present.* Philadelphia, 1918. *Bib.*
302. Lang, A. *Myth, Ritual and Religion.* London, 1901.
307. Murray, G. *Four Stages of Greek Religion.* New York, 1912.
308. Harrison, J. E. *Themis.* Cambridge, 1912.
309. —— *Prolegomena to Greek Religion.* Cambridge, 1903.

CULT OF GODDESS AND MOTHER-RIGHT

O, Index "Maternal descent"; B, II, 584.
315. Farnell, L. R. *Greece and Babylon.* Edinburgh, 1911, chap. V.
316. Dietrich, R. *Muttererde.* Berlin, 1905.
317. Frazer, J. G. *Adonis, Attis, Osiris, Studies in History of Oriental Religion.* London, 1906. See Index, "Mother-right."
318. Hartley, C. G. (Mrs. W. M. Gallichan). *The Position of Woman in Primitive Society.* London, 1914.
319. Bennett, F. M. "Religious Cults Associated with Amazons," *Col. Univ. Press.* New York, 1912.
320. Reinach, S. "La Station néolithique," *Le Jablanica l'Anth.,* 1901, 333.
321. Smith, W. R. *Kinship and Marriage in Early Arabia.* Cambridge, 1885.
322. Mannhard, W. *Wald- und Feld-kulte.* 2d ed. Berlin, 1905.
323. Helms, K. *Altgermanische Religionsgeschichte.* Heidelberg, 1913, I. Cf. **179**, 93.
325. Ellis, H. *Man and Woman.* London, 1894. Cf. 4th ed., 1917.

CHAPTER XI—PROGRESS

335. Marvin, F. S., Editor. *Unity of Western Civilization.* London, 1915.
336. —— *Progress and History.* London, 1916.
337. —— *The Living Past.* 2d ed. Oxford, 1915.
338. Murray, G. *Religio Grammatici.* Boston, 1918.

CHAPTER XII—THE COMING OF THE INDO-EUROPEANS

340. Müller, F. Max. *Biographies of Words and Home of Aryans.* London, 1888.
341. Meillet, A. *Les Langues dans l'Europe nouvelle.* Paris, 1918.
342. —— *Les Dialectes Indo-européens.* Paris, 1908.
343. —— *Introduction à l'Étude comparative des Langues Indo-européennes.* 4th ed. Paris, 1915.
346. Meyer, E. *Geschichte des Alterthums.* 2d ed. Stuttgart, 1909. Vol. I, Pt. 2, p. 722.
347. Schrader, O. *Reallexikon der indogermanischen Alterthumskunde.* Strassburg, 1902.
348. —— *Sprachvergleichung und Urgeschichte.* 3d ed. Jena, 1906.
349. —— *Die Indogermanen.* Leipsic, 1911, 165 pp.
—— (Trans. Jevons, F. B.) *Prehistoric Antiquities of the Aryan Peoples.* London, 1890.
350. Feist, S. *Kultur. Ausbreitung und Herkunft der Indogermanen.* Berlin, 1913.
351. —— *Europa im Lichte der Vorgeschichte.* Berlin, 1910.
352. Hirt, H. *Die Indogermanen.* 2 vols. Strassburg, 1905–07.
353. Kossina, G. "Die indogermanische Frage archäologisch beantwortet," *Zts. f. Eth.,* XXXIV (1902), 161, N. B. Cf. 220.
354. Much, M. *Heimat der Indogermanen.* 2d ed. Berlin, 1904.
355. Reinach, S. *Origine des Aryens.* Paris, 1892.
356. Wilser, L. *Die Germanen.* Leipsic, 1903.

357. —— *Herkunft und Urgeschichte der Arier.* Heidelberg, 1899.

358. Zaborowski, Moindron S. "La Patrie originaire des Aryens," *R. E. A.* Paris, XIII (1903), 253.

359. —— *Les Peuples aryens d'Asie et d'Europe.* Paris, 1908.

360. Brunnhofer, G. H. *Arische Urzeit.* Bern, 1909.

361. Laponge, G. V. de. *L'Aryen, Son Rôle social.* Paris, 1899.

362. Hehn, V. *Kulturpflanzen und Hausthiere.* 5th ed. Berlin, 1887.

363. Holmes, T. R. *Ancient Britain.* Oxford, 1907. Chap. III and pp. 424–455.

364. Veblen, T. *Imperial Germany and the Industrial Revolution.* New York, 1915.

365. Huntington, E. *The Pulse of Asia.* Boston, 1911.

366. —— *Palestine and Its Transformations.* Boston, 1907.

367. —— *World Power and Evolution.* New Haven, 1919.

375. Murray, G. *Euripides and His Age.* New York, 1913.

376. Chesterton, G. K. *Charles Dickens.* London, 1917.

377. Lang, A. *Custom and Myth.* New York, 1885.

378. Gummere, F. B. *The Beginnings of Poetry.* New York, 1901.

INDEX